HOW A
STEAM LOCOMOTIVE
WORKS

HOW A
STEAM LOCOMOTIVE
WORKS

DOMINIC WELLS

Ian Allan
PUBLISHING

Acknowledgements

The author would like to acknowledge the following individuals and organisations for their varied assistance whilst producing this book.

For providing the crucial inspiration to write the book, Peter Lawson.

For proofreading the various drafts, Paul Davies, Catherine Lawson, Peter Levick, Ian Screeton and Daniel Wells.

For providing suggestions on specific chapters, James King, Shaun McMahon and Murray Reid.

For reproduction of all the illustrations, Richard Wells.

For photographic advice and assistance, Bernard Dixon and Richard Filimon.

For providing behind-the-scenes access, the following organisations, their staff and volunteers: the Festiniog and Welsh Highland Railways, the Great Central Railway, The A1 Steam Locomotive Trust and Tyseley Locomotive Works.

For allowing and assisting behind-the-scenes access, John Bell, Alan Binder, James Hazell, Alan James, Alastair Meanley, Bob Meanley, Graham Pattison and Rob Stinchcombe.

First published 2010

ISBN 978 0 7110 3434 1

Published by Ian Allan Publishing

an imprint of Ian Allan Publishing Ltd, Hersham, Surrey, KT12 4RG
Printed in England by Ian Allan Printing Ltd, Hersham, Surrey, KT12 4RG

Distributed in Canada and the United States of America by BookMasters Distribution Services

Code: 1004/x

Visit the Ian Allan Publishing website at www.ianallanpublishing.com

Mixed Sources
Product group from well-managed forests and other controlled sources
www.fsc.org Cert no. SGS-COC-005526
© 1996 Forest Stewardship Council
FSC

Contents

Foreword

If I were to say 'everyone's fascinated by steam locomotives', that might tell you more about the company I tend to keep than human nature itself. But, working on one of Britain's leading heritage railways, training and managing footplate crews, the majority of people I meet – whether volunteers giving up their weekends and holiday leave to work on (mend, drive or fire) steam locomotives, or members of the public taking pictures of them or paying to ride behind them – seem to be anything from curious about them to mesmerised by them. Why? Is there not something primæval about them, something you'd think would be in Genesis Chapter 1? Yes, steam (*anything* steam) stimulates people's memories (of childhood, or the 'good old days') and their knowledge of raw scientific principles like no other machine. But the briefest of chats with first-time volunteers – certainly with most passengers – usually reveals at best only a *basic* knowledge of how steam locomotives work; 'fire boils water makes steam makes the wheels go round' is where most of them are. The rest of it – that's secret.

Dominic Wells knows this only too well. But he knows the secrets too. And he knows how to unfold them, how to explain those little mysteries, how to unravel those things which baffle the baffled! Happily (for anyone who buys this book) he's uniquely qualified to do so, having gained locomotive footplate experience on the 2ft-gauge Welsh Highland Railway, where both oil and coal are used as fuels; on the 15in Kirklees Light Railway in West Yorkshire and as a fully qualified Mechanical Engineer at the former LNER Doncaster Works. He has a full range of experience of railway locomotives – large, medium and small, steam, diesel or electric – not to mention the things they haul around behind them (*i.e.* carriages and wagons) and the track on which they run. Moreover, he's keen to share his knowledge and experience with others, and is particularly good at doing so. So the reader's in good hands!

On top of all that, he's not a stuck-in-the-past heritage buff prone to utterances such as "'A3s' look awful with German smoke-deflectors", "All this station needs is a few milk churns and porters' barrows to look like the real thing" or "A Standard 4 tank can easily do the ton!" No pointless nostalgia here, no blind adherence to yesteryear. After all, a good many of today's tourist railways are in the entertainment business, where it's important to make money, where safety, efficiency and professionalism are everything, and the 'right' colour or valve-wheel pattern is immaterial. Refreshingly, Dominic's is a new outlook. Not for him yet another reincarnation or regurgitation of the BR Black Book (the 'Handbook for Railway Steam Locomotive Enginemen') – positively biblical though that was (and still is) in its authority and wisdom. Dominic is keen on steam locomotives being looked after, being improved and 'tuned' to peak efficiency, being understood, and operated and maintained by sympathetic *knowing* crews – and their secrets being revealed. And he's keen on involving a new generation – youngsters who never 'knew' steam and who've probably never had a coal fire in their lounge.

So this book IS different. I hope you admire (as I do) Dominic's excellent computer drawings and find them helpful – models of clarity? Yes! I trust you'll find his excursions outside Black Book territory (things like air brakes, oil firing and articulated locomotives) stimulating and useful. And, given his gift for explaining difficult or complicated components and scientific principles in a palatable and digestible way, I feel this book is likely to appeal at *all* levels – to experienced footplatemen as well as beginners. Of course that's important, because no machine remains forever mysterious quite like the steam locomotive. Any driver or fireman will confirm that! You can have a lifetime's work behind you, or drive them several thousand miles a year, and *still* be baffled by their schizophrenic disposition (steaming well on one trip, and not at all the next!), by their irritating faults, and their refusal to be diagnosed, by their intermittent noises and hotspots – their secrets!

Granted, it's a cliché (among steam buffs at least), but it's true: you can't drive or fire a steam locomotive like you drive a car. You've got to *know* what you're doing – what happens when you put coal *there* rather than *here*; when you open this valve fully rather than part-way; when you notch up three rather than two; when you tighten this up one turn or two; whether you should sand *here* or oil *there*.

Mastering steam locomotives requires knowledge, understanding and experience; one's no good without the others. Hopefully this book will help with two of these three pre-requisites. All I can say is "Good luck with the third!"

Peter Lawson
Locomotive Crew Supervisor
Ffestiniog and Welsh Highland Railways

Introduction

There are now many steam railways in the UK, and there is much interest in the steam locomotive. Steam-railway volunteers and enthusiasts come from all walks of life and often do not have either an engineering or a railway background. Therefore, the process of learning about the steam locomotive, or acquiring the knowledge to work on steam railways, can sometimes take considerable time.

It is hoped that this book will provide simple answers for as wide a range of readers as possible, whether he/she be an active railway volunteer or an enthusiast wanting to know how the steam locomotive works, and why locomotives take a particular form.

There are many different types of steam locomotive operating in the UK, from standard-gauge express-passenger locomotives to narrow-gauge articulated locomotives. However, all steam locomotives function in the same way, whether they weigh 10 tonnes or 100 tonnes.

The steam locomotive is sometimes described as a simple machine, because it has fewer parts than more modern forms of traction. However, the engineering of steam locomotives can be very complex, due largely to the way in which all the constituent parts have to interact within a limited space.

This book provides an explanation of the steam locomotive by use of a large number of easily understandable diagrams, explaining the function of the components in a step-by-step manner.

The steam locomotive is a fascinating, exciting machine, and gaining a better understanding of how it works is very fulfilling, especially for an aspiring driver or fireman. Hopefully this book will provide a good foundation for any reader wishing to understand the subject.

Dominic Wells
MEng CEng MIMechE

Chapter 1

Steam Power and Boilers

Steam power

The steam locomotive is fundamentally different from a kettle. To understand this difference, we will examine how a kettle would have to be modified to turn it into a steam-engine boiler. **Figure 1.1** shows a kettle in the form of a simple drum. Inside the kettle is water and underneath the kettle is a fire. The fire heats the bottom of the kettle and this heat is absorbed by the water. This heating of the water turns it gradually into steam. When heated, water like any other liquid will turn into gas and in doing so, it expands. When the water in this kettle turns into steam, the steam (gas) rises and appears to be generated at the surface, much like in the household k ettle. The steam wants to take up more room as it expands, so it eventually escapes out of the top of the kettle. If the fire was maintained indefinitely, the water level would gradually fall, as the water is converted into steam. Eventually the water would run dry, and the heat from the fire would burn and possibly melt the base of the kettle.

If we want to make use of steam to push pistons inside cylinders and thus turn wheels and do useful work, it needs to have pressure much like using compressed air. To achieve this with the kettle, it is necessary to seal the top shut as shown in **Figure 1.2**, so that the steam cannot escape. Now when the fire heats the water and generates steam, the steam cannot expand. It has to remain in the limited space at the top of the kettle. This causes it to pressurise. If the fire was maintained indefinitely, more and more steam would be created, but without any increase in space the pressure of the steam will rise. Eventually the pressure would become so great that it would burst the kettle, causing an explosion. The amount that the pressure would have to rise to cause this to happen would depend on the strength designed into the container, now referred to as a boiler and not a kettle. However, there is a limit to how much pressure can be accommodated in

Figure 1.1
A simple kettle

Figure 1.2
Kettle with lid sealed

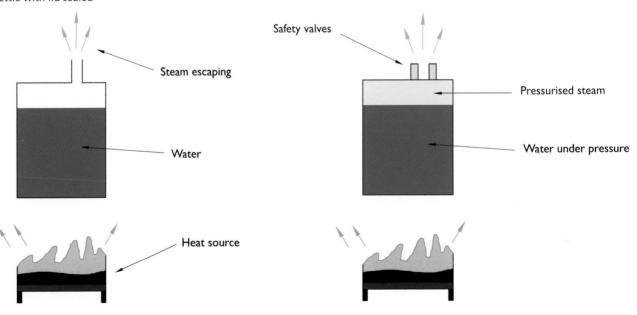

Steam escaping

Safety valves

Pressurised steam

Water

Water under pressure

Heat source

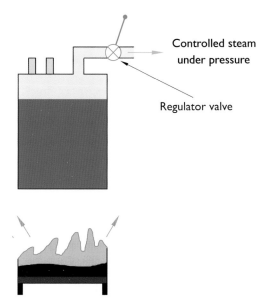

Figure 1.3
A simple boiler

work the valve. Our boiler now has a means of being used for useful work, and has seemingly been prevented from explosion under high steam pressure. However, if the fire is maintained indefinitely and the steam continues to be used to do work by being allowed past the regulator valve, then the water will eventually run out. When all that remains inside the boiler is pressurised steam, the heat from the fire would burn and possibly melt the base of the boiler, as the steam will not be able to absorb the heat as effectively as the water. Unlike the kettle, the burning of the base of this boiler could weaken it so that it will explode under reduced steam pressures.

The boiler as described so far could only be used for a limited length of time, as the water will eventually run out. Therefore, to continue to use this boiler for hours on end, we need to supply it with more water. However, we cannot simply pour water into the boiler, because as soon as we open any lid the pressurised steam will be forced out of the boiler in a jet of escaping steam. This would be identical to the effect seen when the safety valves lift. Thus, we could drop the pressure of the boiler to zero by wasting steam and raise it again after water has been poured in, which would waste energy and take considerable time. There is an alternative however, and that is to force water into the boiler under pressure, as shown in **Figure 1.4**.

Figure 1.4
Simple boiler with
water feed

practical terms. Therefore, an important device is added to all boilers, known as a safety valve. Usually this is a valve held shut by a spring of suitable strength. When the pressure rises to the point where it is not desirable for it to rise further (because it would compromise the strength of the boiler) the pressure will overcome the spring and force open the safety valve. Steam will then be allowed to escape and will effectively stop the pressure from rising further than is desired. When the pressure falls, the spring will close the safety valve. The operation of the safety valve is automatic, and all boilers have at least two of them to provide additional safety. Further details on safety valves are provided in Chapter 11.

Having now been able to pressurise steam, we will want to use it as and when required, for example to move a train. To do this we add a pipe from the boiler to where we want to use it (typically pushing the pistons inside cylinders, which we can convert to rotary motion), as shown in **Figure 1.3**. However, we do not usually want to use the steam at a constant rate. In a locomotive we need steam only to start the train, climb hills and counter the effect of resistances. Therefore, our boiler requires another fitting known as a regulator valve. This gives the user the ability to allow steam out of the boiler as and when required. A handle is attached to allow the operator to

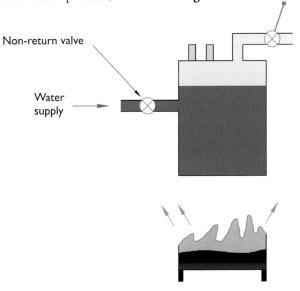

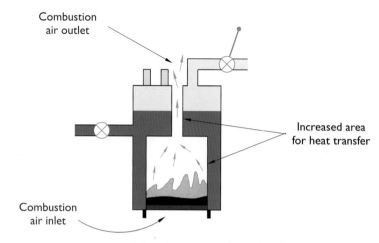

Figure 1.5
Verticle boiler

steam boiler. The boiler illustrated in **Figure 1.4** is essentially the same as any steam locomotive or traction engine boiler in its operation. However, it will not raise steam very quickly, because the only area of heat transfer from the fire to the water is through the base of the boiler.

Basic boilers

On steam locomotives space is limited but there is a large demand for power, so it is necessary to try and make steam locomotive boilers transfer heat as effectively as possible for their limited size. We will now do this with the simple boiler described in the previous section. **Figure 1.5** shows that we now make our boiler hollow so that the fire can be placed inside the cavity. The pressurised water is now contained in the area surrounding the fire. This development has created more surface area, now above and around the fire, for heat transfer to take place. Also, note that the gases from the fire have to be given a free passage to exhaust to atmosphere; otherwise the fire will be choked and will go out. These hot gases pass up a pipe in the boiler, which provides even more area for heat transfer to take place. It is clear from the diagram that we must now keep the level of water much higher, by more regularly forcing water into the boiler, to avoid uncovering the very hot plate of material above the fire. Note that it is not critical to keep water around the exhaust pipe, as the hot gases from the fire cool down as they pass through it. This gas is in effect transferring its heat into the boiler and is not sufficiently hot to damage the structure of the boiler.

The devices used to do this are known as injectors, and these are detailed in Chapter 4. It is important to note that we only need to put water into the boiler when it runs low. We do not need to put water into the boiler continuously, as we are not using the steam all the time. This creates a problem, because when we are not forcing water into the boiler through a suitable pipe, the pressurised water contained in the boiler will want to escape back down this pipe. To prevent this escape, which would drain the boiler of its water, we use a non-return valve, referred to on steam locomotive boilers as a clack valve. This valve is simple in operation, as it is held shut by the pressure in the boiler. When we force water through the pipe into the boiler, the valve is simply lifted from its seat to allow water past. Further details on the different types of valve are provided in Chapter 11.

The above descriptions have shown the fundamental difference between a kettle and a

The cavity containing the fire is known in locomotive terms as the firebox. The wall that separates the fire from the water is known as the inner wall of the firebox. The wall that separates the water from the surroundings is known as the outer wall of the firebox.

To keep the fire going it requires fresh fuel to be added. It is possible in the boiler of Figure 1.5 to supply fresh fuel down the pipe from the top of the boiler. However, it would be difficult to keep the fire even, so closer access to the fire can be provided by a firehole,

Figure 1.6
Verticle boiler with fire hole

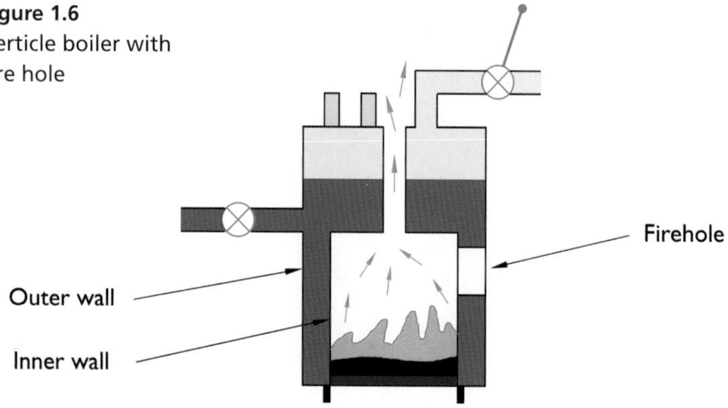

as shown in **Figure 1.6**. This is a large open passage between the outer wall and inner wall of the firebox, and the water can freely circulate around the sides of it.

We can go a step further in improving the efficiency of this boiler, by adding multiple tubes for the hot gases to pass through the top of the boiler, as shown in **Figure 1.7**. The use of many smaller tubes instead of one large tube gives an even greater area for heat transfer to take place. Note once again that it is important to keep the level of water in the boiler covering the firebox. Also note the use of a smokebox to collect the exhaust gases and the chimney to take the exhaust gases up in the air, away from the operator/driver, before discharging them. This boiler is now very close to the design of a traditional vertical boiler.

Locomotive boilers

Whilst the vertical boiler is a very effective generator of steam, it has an important limitation. Trains are limited in height and in width by surrounding structures, such as tunnels and over-bridges. Therefore, it would not be possible to have a very large vertical boiler on a steam locomotive, as it would not fit through such obstacles. Locomotives are not quite so limited in length. Therefore it is much more practical for the steam locomotive boiler to be horizontal and in line with the track.

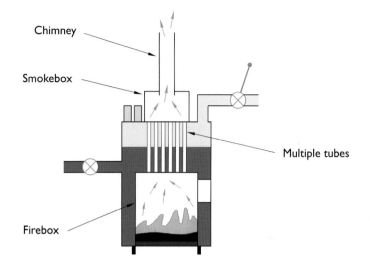

Figure 1.7
Refined verticle boiler

However, this does require it to take a slightly different form to the vertical boiler, as now shown in **Figure 1.8**. All the basic components are the same as previously explained but are now positioned differently.

The gases of the fire now have to pass horizontally through the tubes to the smokebox. The gases will not naturally do this. The fire will simply discharge flames through the firehole and into the cab, in search of air. Therefore, to overcome this problem and ensure that the gases from the fire are drawn along the tubes to the smokebox, a forced draught is generated by a device known as the blastpipe, as shown in **Figure 1.9**. Steam that has been used in the cylinders and is at low pressure is exhausted to the chimney through the blastpipe, which

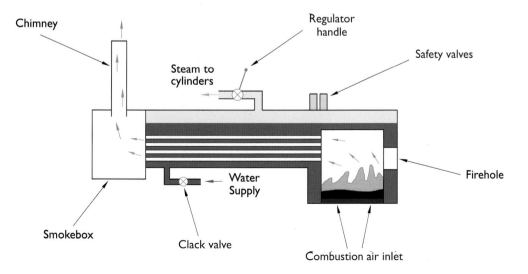

Figure 1.8
Basic locomotive boiler

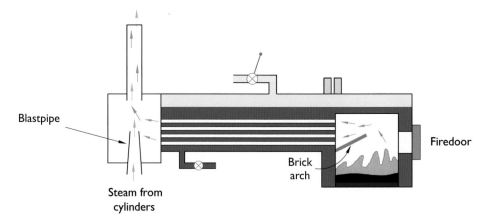

Figure 1.9
Blast pipe, brick arch and firedoor

squeezes it and thus speeds it up. The steam passes through the smokebox and up the chimney, which displaces air from the smokebox and generates suction (vacuum). This suction draws the gases from the fire along the tubes of the boiler. As the locomotive works harder and faster, the jet of steam from the blastpipe is made stronger, thus increasing the vacuum in the smokebox. In this way, the steam locomotive is automatic, the harder it works, the more air is pulled through the fire, making it burn more quickly to generate the required steam.

To allow more time for the gases from the fire to burn fully – and hence reduce the amount of smoke emitted from the chimney – the firebox is typically fitted with an internal wall. This is called the 'brick arch', although it is not always made from firebrick. The purpose of the brick arch is to provide a longer passage from the fire to the boiler tubes, and therefore provide more time for the combustion of the gases to take place.

To ensure that air is drawn through the fire from underneath, rather than over the top through the firehole, the latter is fitted with a door. This can be opened when adding fuel to the fire, and closed for the remainder of the time. The firedoor also prevents flames from being emitted into the cab when there is no vacuum in the smokebox.

The brick arch and the firedoor are also illustrated in **Figure 1.9**.

The steam generated by the boiler will condense and lose its pressure when it cools down. Therefore, to keep the steam as hot as possible on its way to the cylinders, the main steam pipe tends to be located within the boiler itself. From the boiler the steam is conveyed in pipes through the smokebox and to the cylinders, which are typically very close to the underside of the smokebox. If this internal main steam pipe was fitted into the top of the boiler, it would be very close to the water level. This would make it prone to draw

Figure 1.10
Dome and internal main steam pipe

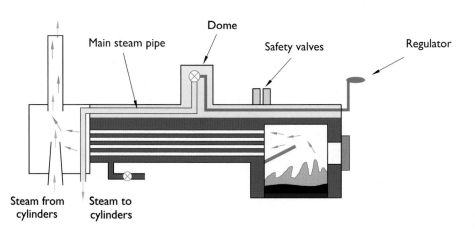

water from the boiler to the cylinders, a process known as 'priming'. Such water would be hazardous to the operation of the cylinders, as demonstrated in a later chapter. Therefore, the boiler is fitted with a vertical extension called the 'dome', as shown in **Figure 1.10**. The dome enables the main steam pipe to collect steam well away from the water level.

The regulator valve is commonly fitted to this end of the main steam pipe (within the dome), and it is operated by linkages from the regulator handle at the back of the boiler.

The ideal shape of any pressure vessel, like the locomotive boiler, is either spherical, or tubular with domed ends. This is verified by the shape adopted by a balloon when it is inflated and can be seen in the form of the common fire extinguisher. The generally tubular shape of the locomotive boiler is therefore ideal to accommodate high pressures, but there are also areas of the boiler that have to be flat. These include the end plates of the boiler and the walls of the firebox. If unsupported, these walls would bulge under the high pressures, and their strength would be compromised. To prevent this from happening, locomotive boilers are fitted with a large number of internal rods, which are fastened between the straight walls to hold them together. These rods are known as stays. A cross-sectional view of a locomotive firebox will reveal a large number of stays, as shown in **Figure 1.11**. These stays hold the outer and inner walls of the firebox together so that they

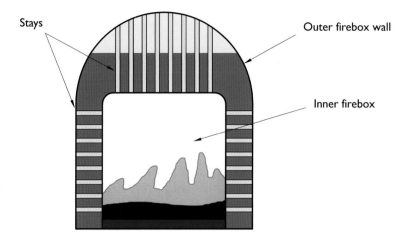
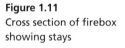

do not bulge under the pressure of the water in the boiler between them.

The exact design and layout of boilers differs between types of locomotives, but the basic function and the components used are the same. **Figure 1.12** shows a typical locomotive boiler.

Associated with every boiler are some vital fittings, which enable the operator to determine the water level and also to replenish it. These fittings are described in detail in the following chapter.

Before finishing this chapter, mention must be made of the boiler-pressure gauge. To get the best possible performance from the locomotive, the crew need to keep the boiler pressure as high as possible. Increasing the pressure will increase the force that the cylinders can provide to the wheels. Therefore, all boilers are fitted with a mechanical gauge to indicate the boiler pressure.

Figure 1.11
Cross section of firebox showing stays

Figure 1.12
This is a typical steam-locomotive boiler, seen without insulation or external cladding. Notice the flange for mounting the dome and also the ends of the numerous stays at the firebox end.

Chapter 2

Water Management

Gauge glasses

In the first chapter it was shown that the effective and safe operation of steam locomotives depends on keeping the water in the boiler at the correct level. To allow the crew to 'see' the water level inside the highly pressurised boiler is a fitting known as the gauge glass. **Figure 2.1** shows the components that make up a gauge glass.

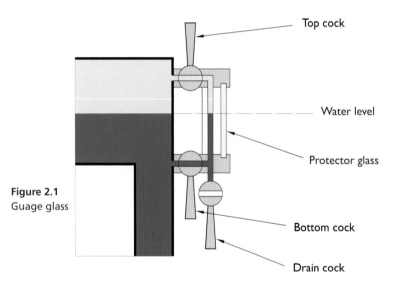

Figure 2.1
Guage glass

Top cock

Water level

Protector glass

Bottom cock

Drain cock

Figure 2.2
When the water is clean it can sometimes be difficult to view the level in a gauge glass. To overcome this, a striped plate is often fitted. As seen in the photo, the water refracts the light so that the stripes change direction.

In normal operation the gauge glasses are set with the top and bottom cock both open, and the drain cock closed. Thus, the driver can deduce the level of water in the boiler from the level in the gauge glass, as illustrated in **Figure 2.2**. This is, of course, provided that the water level is lower than the top cock and higher than the bottom cock.

If the water level is allowed to fall below the bottom cock fitting, the firebox roof (also known as the crown) could become uncovered by water. This could lead to the firebox roof overheating and in a severe situation collapsing, as the structural strength is affected by extreme heat.

If the water level is allowed to build up higher than the top cock fitting, then there is a danger of the locomotive priming. If the water level gets too close to the point where steam is taken to the cylinders (usually the dome), then there is the possibility that water will be sucked into the steam pipe and thus into the cylinders. As part of the cycle of the pistons in the cylinders is compressive, and water is not compressible, damage can result from priming.

The gauge glasses are vital to managing the boiler water level, but it should be clearly understood that they can give false readings if not used correctly. For example, if the top cock was not opened fully (as shown in **Figure 2.3**) then changes in the boiler pressure combined with condensing of the trapped steam could cause the gauge glass to show a higher water level than that actually in the boiler.

Besides incorrect setting of the gauge glass, a false reading can also result from general debris in the water causing a blockage in the narrow passages of the top and bottom cocks. However, such blockages can be removed by blowing through the gauge glass. It is good practice to blow through the gauge glasses before taking a locomotive off shed at the start

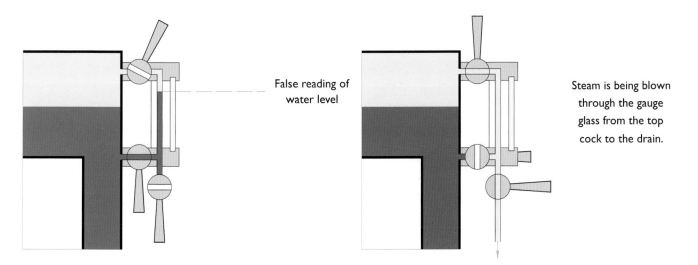

False reading of
water level

Steam is being blown
through the gauge
glass from the top
cock to the drain.

of each day of operation.

The procedure for blowing through the gauge glasses is as follows:

1. Shut top cock and bottom cock.

2. Open drain cock.

3. Open top cock to blow through (see Figure 2.4), then close again.

4. Open bottom cock to blow through then close again.

5. Shut drain cock.

6. Open top and bottom cocks; the water should rise to level.

Although it is a rare occurrence, a gauge glass can burst, and for this reason the fitting has a protector glass (shown in Figure 2.1) to prevent shards of glass from injuring the crew. In the event of a gauge glass burst, the crew will immediately close the top and bottom cocks to stop the escape of steam. The escape of water from the bottom cock flashes instantly into steam when it meets the surrounding atmosphere, and thus produces a much greater volume of steam than that from the top cock. Therefore, the bottom cock fitting commonly has an internal ball to restrict the flow.

For certain locomotive boilers there is a useful additional function that gauge glasses can perform, which is applied when filling up the boiler at the end of the locomotive's turn of duty. As the water will contract slightly

when it cools, and also a small amount of water will be lost as steam leaks during the night, it is necessary to ensure a good level of water is present in the boiler before disposing of the locomotive. To allow the crew to take the water level slightly higher than the visible part of the gauge glass, the bottom cock is isolated and the drain cock opened for a few seconds to evacuate the water. In this setting, shown in **Figure 2.5**, the driver can ascertain when the water level reaches the top cock fitting, as water will begin to trickle into the gauge glass slowly from the top.

There is an added complication in using the gauge glasses on railways with significant gradients. To appreciate the complication the following illustrations will be of use. **Figure 2.6** shows that on level track the reading in the

Figure 2.3
Guage glass incorrectly set

Figure 2.4
Blowing through the top cock

Figure 2.5
Setting to use when filling the boiler

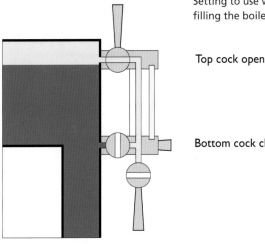

Top cock open

Bottom cock closed

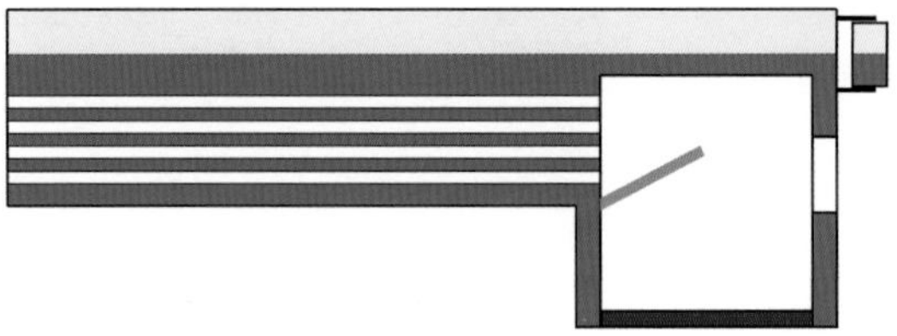

Figure 2.6
Boiler on level track

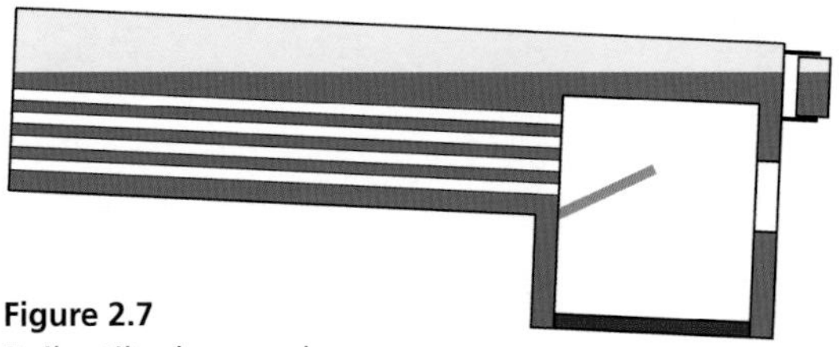

gauge glasses appears exactly as the water level in the boiler. However, when the locomotive points up a gradient, the tilting of the boiler causes the gauge glasses to give a higher reading than the overall water level in the boiler, as

simply stop valves, which when opened let a fine amount of steam or water out of the boiler, as shown in **Figure 2.9**.

One of the try cocks replaces the top fitting of the gauge glass whilst the other replaces the bottom fitting of the gauge glass, as shown in **Figure 2.10**. The fireman must keep the boiler water level between the two cocks, so that when they are opened steam is emitted from the top cock and water is emitted from the bottom cock.

Try cocks can be difficult to use, because the hot water from the boiler tends to flash instantly to steam when it meets the surrounding atmosphere. To determine whether water or steam is being emitted, the cocks should only be opened by the minimum possible amount. This will reduce the tendency of the water to flash into clouds of steam.

Glasses read normal

Figure 2.7
Boiler tilted upwards

Glasses read high

shown in **Figure 2.7**.

When the locomotive points down a gradient the opposite effect occurs. The gauge glasses will give a lower reading than the overall water level in the boiler, as shown in **Figure 2.8**.

The driver and fireman must be familiar with the gradients on the railway so as to be

Fusible plugs

The fusible plug is a device fitted in the top of the firebox, which provides a final warning to the crew in the event of the water falling below a safe level. The fusible plug has the fire below it and the water above it, as shown in **Figure 2.11**. The centre part of the fitting is filled with lead.

If the water level falls below the top of the firebox the lead will melt, and then steam will escape from the boiler into the firebox, as shown in **Figure 2.12**. This provides a warning to the crew before the integrity of the firebox roof becomes compromised. The crew should immediately turn on both injectors and/or feed pumps (see Chapter 3) and put out the fire.

Glasses read low

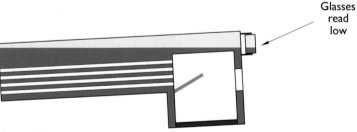

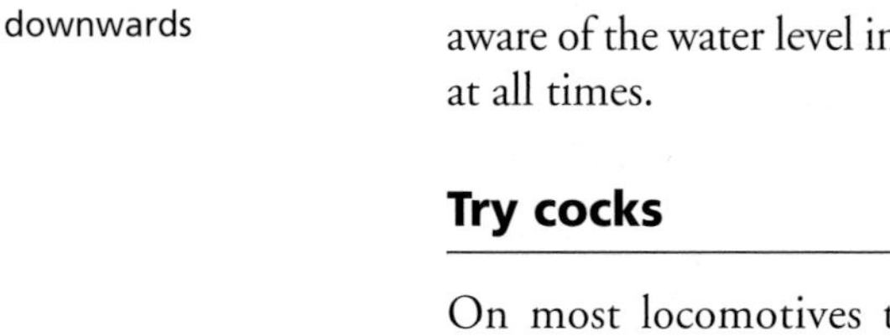

Figure 2.8
Boiler tilted downwards

aware of the water level in the boiler accurately at all times.

Try cocks

On most locomotives there are two gauge glasses. However, on some locomotives there is only a single gauge glass, which is supplemented by try cocks. The try cocks are

Water impurities

Water used in steam locomotives is not special. It contains impurities, which accumulate as solids on the walls of the boiler, as illustrated in **Figure 2.13**. In the early days of steam locomotives this problem was not understood, and quickly proved hazardous. The build-up of solids, particularly around the firebox, reduces the cooling effect of the water

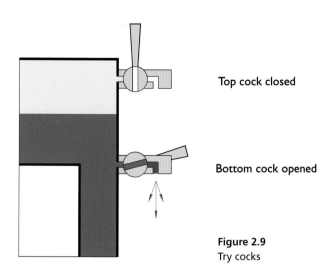

Figure 2.9
Try cocks

on the boiler plates. In extreme circumstances the plates can overheat and lose their structural integrity. Thus, since the early days of locomotives, boilers have evolved to make it possible to gain access to the vulnerable areas and clear the solids away.

Wash-outs

All modern boilers are fitted with wash-out plugs. These are fixed in the boiler by screw threads and are removed once there is no steam pressure, leaving small access holes. Before a wash-out the boiler is emptied, as shown in **Figure 2.14**. The small access holes are then used to insert special water hoses, which have nozzles on the end in order to create a powerful jet of water. By directing such jets of water around the boiler, built-up solids can be effectively dislodged. The resulting sludge is drained from the boiler at the lowest access hole. Rods can also be inserted through the access holes to scrape away the solids.

The procedure for carrying out a wash-out, with the locomotive not in steam, is as follows:

1. Check that there is no steam pressure in the boiler.

2. Open the blow-down valve (described below) to drain the water.

3. Open the regulator and check that the cylinder drains are open, to allow air

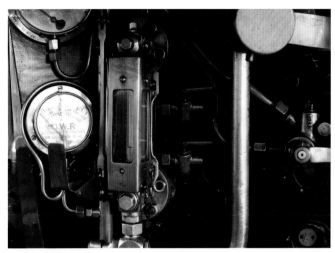

Figure 2.10
On former Great Western Railway locomotives a single gauge-glass fitting is backed up by adjacent try cocks. In the event of the gauge glass's bursting (and subsequently being isolated) the safe level of water in the boiler can be determined by opening the try cocks.

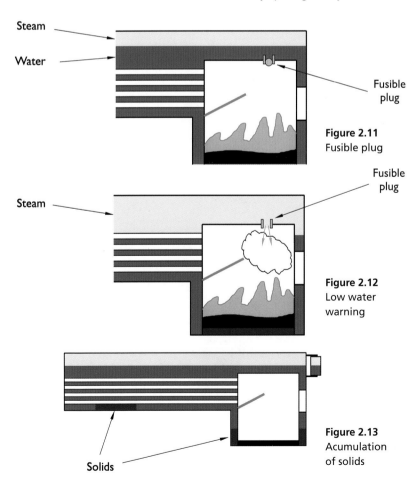

Steam
Water

Fusible plug

Figure 2.11
Fusible plug

Fusible plug

Steam

Figure 2.12
Low water warning

Figure 2.13
Acumulation of solids

Solids

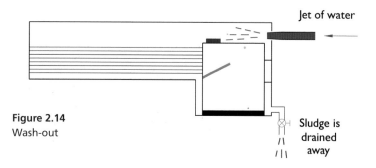

Figure 2.14
Wash-out

into the boiler, otherwise water cannot empty from the boiler.

4. Remove the wash-out plugs.

5. Use the water hose and nozzles to scour away the sludge from inside the boiler. Note that there are usually two nozzles, one is a straight nozzle, and the other is curved for accessing awkward areas.

6. Refit the wash-out plugs and close the blow-down valve.

7. Fill the boiler with water.

8. Close the regulator.

9. Put the locomotive into steam and check for any leaks around the plugs that were removed to carry out the wash-out.

In addition to boiler washouts there are other methods of reducing the build-up of solids on the inside of boilers. These methods include daily blow-downs and/or water treatment.

Blow-downs

Figure 2.15
Blow-down valve

Blow-downs are carried out by opening a special blow-down valve. This is a valve

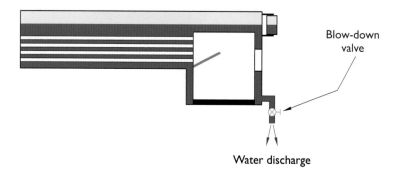

Water discharge

directly connecting the water space around the bottom of the firebox to the outside, as shown in **Figure 2.15**.

When the locomotive is in steam (*i.e.* the boiler is under pressure) and the blow-down valve is opened, water is rapidly discharged from the boiler. This creates a flow of water around the firebox which scours away any newly-formed solids. The water discharged has a high temperature, so it is seen to flash instantly into a cloud of steam when it meets the cold air outside the boiler, as shown in **Figure 2.16**.

Water treatment

To extend the life of the boilers most railways now use water treatment, of which there are two common methods:

1. Eliminate impurities in the water supply before it reaches the locomotives, usually by means of expensive water-treatment plants.

2. Allow impurities in the water to enter the boiler but prevent them from adhering to the boiler plates, by adding chemicals into the locomotive's water tanks.

The latter method tends to be the most common, and it comes in many different specialised forms. With some of the chemical water treatments the impurities are flushed out by daily blow-downs. With other treatments the daily blow-down is eliminated and the impurities are allowed to form into a mobile sludge, which is retained in the boiler for several weeks.

If the chemical water treatments are fully effective, then the wash-out process is simply a means of emptying any accumulated impurities from the boiler. There should be little or no built-up solids on the boiler plates.

One slight disadvantage of using chemical water treatments is an increased likelihood of priming. The chemicals added to the boiler have a tendency to create foam, which can cause the water in the boiler to be drawn into

the main steam pipe. In extreme cases the presence of this incompressible water in the cylinders can burst off the end covers.

If priming is suspected the crew can counteract it in several ways. Easing back on the regulator will reduce the steam demand. This will reduce the drawing of water into the main steam pipe. Opening the cylinder drains will reduce the likelihood of damage to the cylinders. In each case the compromise is to reduce the speed of the train.

If the priming is severe it may be necessary to stop the train and flush out some of the chemicals with the blow-down valve. However, excessive use of the blow-down valve can reduce the effectiveness of the water treatment.

To help prevent priming a small amount of anti-foam is usually added to the boiler with the water treatment. However, this chemical can be

Figure 2.16
This is the spectacular effect of a blow-down. Appropriate care has to be taken as to when and where this operation is carried out.

Chapter 3

Boiler Fittings

Manifold

To provide the steam supply for the various steam fittings, most boilers are fitted with a manifold. This collects steam at the top of the boiler in exactly the same way as the dome. Examples of manifolds are illustrated in **Figures 3.1 and 3.2**.

Blower

When a locomotive is stationary there is no jet of steam from the blastpipe, and therefore no draught to enhance the fire. Opening the blower valve allows steam from the boiler to be sent straight up the chimney via small nozzles, as shown in **Figure 3.3**. Like the blastpipe itself, the blower nozzles displace air from the smokebox and thus generate a draught on the fire.

It is common for blower nozzles to be fitted onto a ring surrounding the blastpipe, as shown in **Figure 3.4**.

Injectors

The purpose of an injector is to replenish the water in the boiler which is being converted to steam to propel the locomotive. The boiler is under pressure, so this pressure must be overcome to add additional water. In the earliest locomotives this was achieved using a pump that was often driven by one of the axles. Thus, these early locomotives had to be moving in order to put water into the boiler. However, the vast majority of steam locomotives later used a device known as an injector.

The injector uses steam from the boiler to force water into the boiler. The layout of the piping associated with the injector is shown in

Figure 3.1
This manifold is situated inside the cab of a GWR locomotive. Notice the various valves and pipes which convey steam to all the auxiliaries. Placing the manifold and pipes inside the cab like this gives the exterior of the locomotive a tidy appearance and makes it easier to keep clean.

Figure 3.2
This manifold is situated outside the cab of a modern Beyer-Garratt locomotive. Notice the operating rods from the cab to the valves on the manifold, and also the various steam pipes leading to the auxiliaries. Placing the hot manifold and pipes outside the cab in this way keeps the cab cool and is safer for the crew should any of the steam fittings fail in an accident.

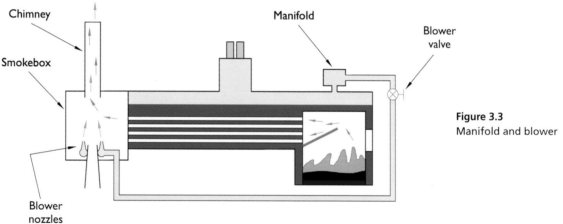

Figure 3.3
Manifold and blower

Figure 3.4
At the base of the smokebox is the blastpipe, in this case with a blower ring mounted around the top. Steam from the boiler is supplied directly to the blower ring by means of the adjacent steam pipe.

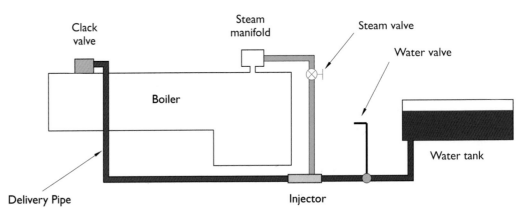

Figure 3.5
Layout of piping

Figure 3.5. Water is released from a tank to flow into the injector under the influence of gravity. A steam valve is then opened to allow steam from the boiler into the injector, where it simultaneously mixes with the water whilst pressurising it to a pressure that is greater than that in the boiler. At this higher pressure the water forces its way along the delivery pipe

steam into mechanical energy to pump water into the boiler. However, the injector performs the task without the need for any moving parts. The injector converts the energy of the pressurised steam into speed energy, known more commonly as kinetic energy. To achieve this conversion of energy a simple cone can be used.

Cones are used to convert energy from pressure into speed or vice-versa, as illustrated in **Figure 3.6**. Anyone who has used a garden hose will be familiar with the fact that the water in the hose (i.e. from the tap) is at high pressure but is not moving very fast. However, the water leaving the hose has no pressure but is moving very fast. This is the work of the cone on the end, converting pressure into speed.

High pressure — Low pressure

Low speed — High speed

Figure 3.6
Function of a cone

and past a non-return valve (known as the clack valve) into the boiler.

Using steam from the boiler to force water back into the boiler initially appears to be unfeasible. However, the engineering principles that make the injector work are actually quite logical.

If the injector was merely a chamber, then the pressure of steam from the boiler would simply equalise with the pressure of water in the delivery pipe, and the water would not move into the boiler. However, if the energy in the pressure of the steam can be converted into a different form of energy, it then becomes possible to use a greater amount of steam from the boiler to force a smaller amount of water into the boiler.

One way of achieving this is to use a steam-powered pump to pressurise the water. This would convert the energy of the pressurised

The above process can be reversed. A jet of water can be sent into the end of a cone and hence into a pipe, where it will pressurise if there is anything resisting its flow.

There are essentially three cones fitted into an injector. These are known as the *steam cone*, the *combining cone* and the *delivery cone*, as shown in **Figure 3.7**.

The first step in the operation of the injector is to open the water feed so that water from the tank (which has no pressure and little speed) is flowing through the combining cone, as shown in **Figure 3.8**. The crew can see this water escaping from the overflow pipe.

The next step is to turn on the steam feed, allowing steam at boiler pressure to enter the steam cone, as illustrated in **Figure 3.9**. In the steam cone the steam loses its pressure and is accelerated to a very high speed.

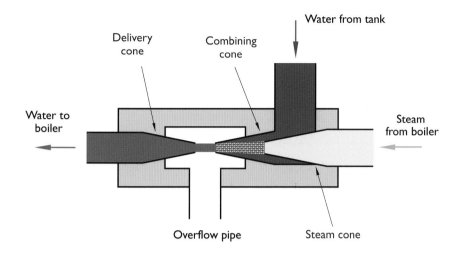

Figure 3.7
Components of a simple injector

Delivery cone

Combining cone

Water from tank

Water to boiler

Steam from boiler

Overflow pipe

Steam cone

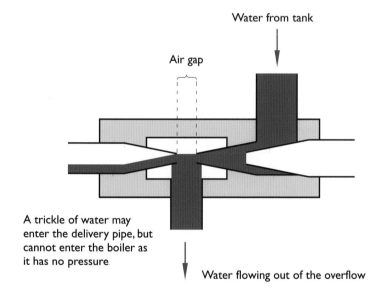

Figure 3.8
Injector with water feed only

Water from tank

Air gap

A trickle of water may enter the delivery pipe, but cannot enter the boiler as it has no pressure.

Water flowing out of the overflow

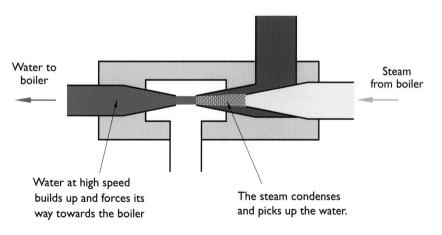

Figure 3.9
Injector with water an steam feed

Water to boiler

Steam from boiler

Water at high speed builds up and forces its way towards the boiler

The steam condenses and picks up the water.

Figure 3.10
Injector at low pressure

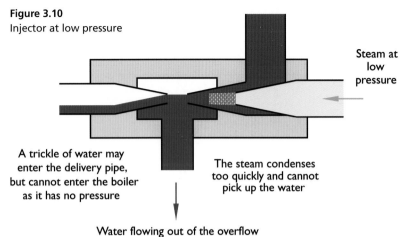

Steam at low pressure

A trickle of water may enter the delivery pipe, but cannot enter the boiler as it has no pressure

The steam condenses too quickly and cannot pick up the water

Water flowing out of the overflow

Figure 3.11
This injector is fitted on a GWR pannier-tank locomotive. The water from the tank flows to the injector through the green pipe, whilst steam is applied through the black pipe from the rear. The resulting pressurised feed water

The resulting jet of steam leaves the steam cone and immediately meets the water from the water tank in the combining cone. The steam is instantly condensed by the cold water, and the mixture of condensed steam and cold water contracts to form a very narrow jet of water. This channels a large amount of energy from the steam into a rapid jet of water, which then bridges the air gap and quickly fills the delivery pipe.

The delivery cone converts the speed of the water jet into pressure. When the pressure is sufficient the water can force its way past the non-return valve (clack valve) and into the boiler.

Note that there is no space now for the cold water to flow out of the combining cone and trickle out of the overflow. It has to become part of the rapid jet.

The purpose of the air gap is to allow excess steam and water to escape during the operation of starting the injector.

If the injector is left running the input of cool water will cause the boiler pressure to fall. This has an impact on the working of the injector. The steam being fed into the steam cone at a lower pressure will become insufficient to pick up as much cold water, because the lower pressure leads to lower speed. Thus the steam jet is condensed too quickly by the cold water and cannot convey it across the air gap to the delivery cone. The combined water and steam now starts trickling away through the overflow pipe, as illustrated in **Figure 3.10**. The solution is to 'trim' (*i.e.* reduce) the water feed, the lower steam pressure becoming sufficient to pick up the smaller quantity of cold water. Note that the injector, when using steam at lower pressure, will have a reduced feed rate. At very low pressures the injector will start to become ineffective. Note that the injector works on logical principles. More energy is used in the input (steam from the boiler) than the work gained at the output (forcing water into the boiler).

The paragraphs above describe the injector in its simplest form. This would be termed a gravity-fed live-steam injector, because the water from the tank flows to it under gravity and the steam is taken directly from the boiler. Injectors are often very easy to identify on the outsides of locomotives, a typical example being illustrated in **Figure 3.11**.

There are some common variations on injector design, and these are described below.

Lifting injectors

On many early locomotives the injectors were conveniently mounted on the back of the boiler (inside the cab), as shown in **Figure 3.12**. In this position water cannot flow under gravity through them as they are higher than the water in the tank.

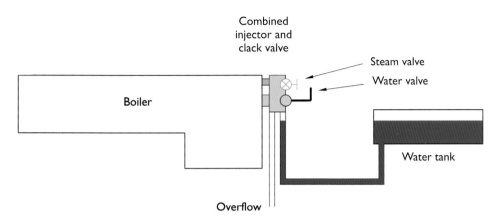

Combined
injector and
clack valve

Steam valve

Water valve

Boiler

Water tank

Overflow

Figure 3.12
Arrangement of
lifting injector

A lifting injector has exactly the same components as the simple gravity fed injector described previously. The only difference is that when starting the lifting injector, the steam passing through the combining cone has to suck the water up to the injector. **Figure 3.13** shows a lifting injector as fitted onto the back of a locomotive boiler.

Exhaust-steam injectors

To improve efficiency the exhaust-steam injector was designed to use some of the exhaust steam from the cylinders instead of live steam from the boiler. This exhaust steam is under pressure as it approaches the blastpipe, but its pressure is less than that of live steam, so the exact design of the injector cones in an exhaust steam injector is different to that of the simple injector described previously. It may be noted that the exhaust steam is available only when the locomotive is working. When the locomotive is standing or is coasting there is no exhaust steam. For this reason exhaust-steam injectors are fitted with a back-up live-steam supply from the boiler. It is the operation of this live steam which starts the injector, but it is used automatically by the injector only when no exhaust steam is

Figure 3.13
This lifting injector is fitted directly onto the back of the boiler, and is higher than the water in the tank. Once the steam valve is opened the steam first has to draw the water up to the injector by vacuum, but then this device functions in exactly the same way as a gravity-fed injector.

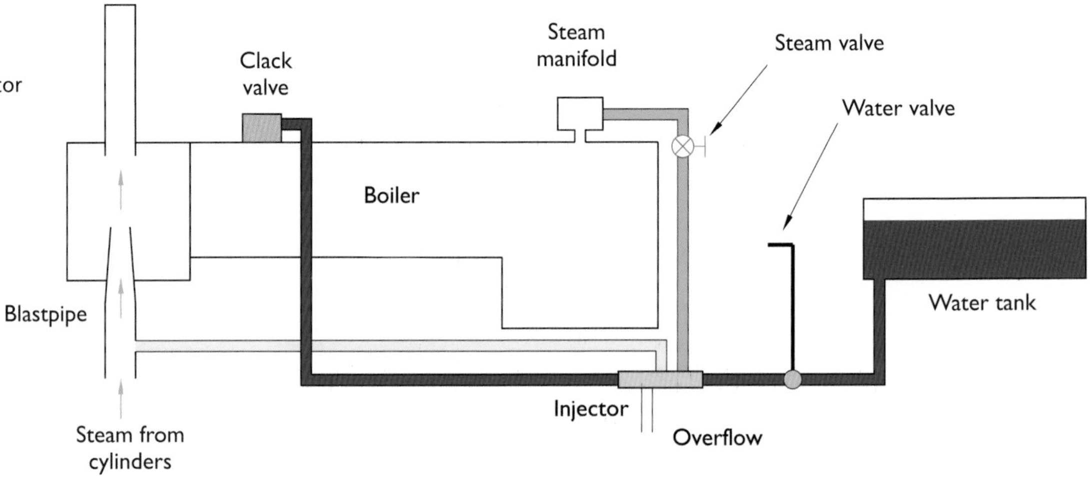

Figure 3.14
Arrangement of
exhaust-steam injector

Steam
manifold

Clack
valve

Steam valve

Water valve

Boiler

Blastpipe

Water tank

Injector

Steam from
cylinders

Overflow

available. **Figure 3.14** illustrates the arrangement of an exhaust-steam injector.

Feed pumps

Besides the different forms of injector, further mention must be made of steam-powered pumps, which are known as feed pumps. These are mechanical devices using either pistons or rotor blades to pressurise the water feed. The power to drive the pumps is provided by steam from the boiler. The most common reason for using a feed pump instead of an injector is because it can pump warm water as well as cold water, whereas an injector will only work with relatively cold water. On modern steam locomotives pre-warming of the feed water is used because it improves the efficiency of the locomotive. However, feed pumps have moving parts that require significantly more maintenance than injectors.

Whether using injectors or feed pumps,

there are always at least two means of forcing water into the boiler, so that each provides a back-up in case one device fails to operate.

Auxiliaries

Slacker pipe

The slacker pipe is a hose with an end nozzle, supplied with pressurised water through a shut-off valve. It is used to spray water over the coal in the tender or bunker, to dampen any coal dust and prevent it from being blown around the footplate. Wetting the coal also has the beneficial effect of keeping coal dust on the fire bed long enough to burn, whereas dry dust will be drawn straight up the chimney by the draught. The slacker pipe can also be used to clean the cab floor. The pressurised water supply usually comes from one of the injectors, as shown in **Figure 3.15**. Thus the slacker pipe can only be used when the

Figure 3.15
Slacker pipe

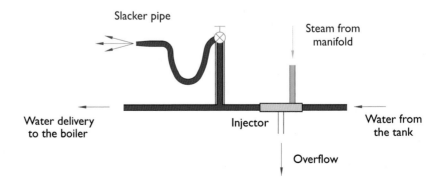

Slacker pipe

Steam from
manifold

Water delivery
to the boiler

Injector

Water from
the tank

Overflow

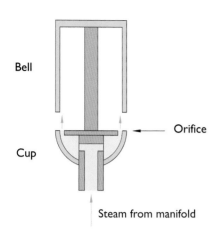

Bell

Cup

Orifice

Steam from manifold

injector is running. When the injector is turned off there is no water supply.

Whistle

The whistle is a warning device, which is used to alert both railwaymen and the general public to the approach of a train. The whistle is typically sounded before a train or locomotive starts to move, and also on approach to level crossings. The device consists of two parts, the cup and the bell. Steam from the boiler is released via a control valve into the cup, from where it emits from an orifice, thence striking the edge of the bell. This is shown in **Figure 3.16**. The actual sound of the whistle depends on the detail design of the basic parts, and some locomotives are fitted with multiple whistles with different tones for different warnings.

Steam heating

During the winter months it is often necessary to provide heating in the carriages. There is more than one way of heating the carriages. For example electric heating can be provided, the electricity being produced by an independent or axle-driven generator on the carriages themselves. However, an alternative system is possible with steam locomotives, and that is to use the locomotive's boiler to supply steam for heating the carriages. Steam is taken from the top of the locomotive's boiler through a controlling and pressure-reducing valve and then into heating pipes that run along the length of the train, as shown in **Figure 3.17**.

The steam demand on the locomotive boiler will be greater when steam heating is being supplied. The end fittings on steam heating pipes get very hot when in use, so care must be taken when disconnecting the hoses between vehicles.

Figure 3.16
Whistle

Figure 3.17
Train with steam heating

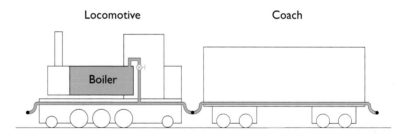

Locomotive

Coach

Boiler

Chapter 4

Combustion

The conventional coal fire

The most common fuel used in steam locomotives is coal. In a conventional coal-fired steam locomotive coal is burned on firebars. There are numerous firebars, with gaps between them, and collectively these are known as the firegrate. The air for combustion is drawn up

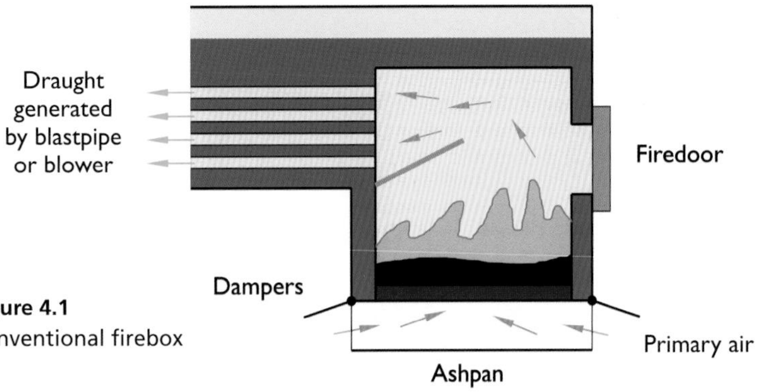

Figure 4.1
Conventional firebox

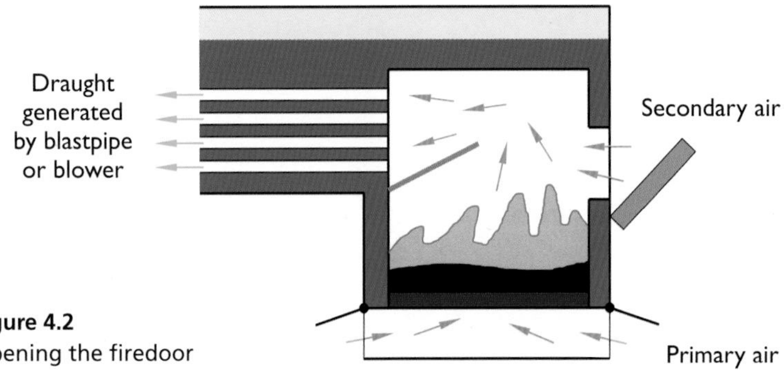

Figure 4.2
Opening the firedoor

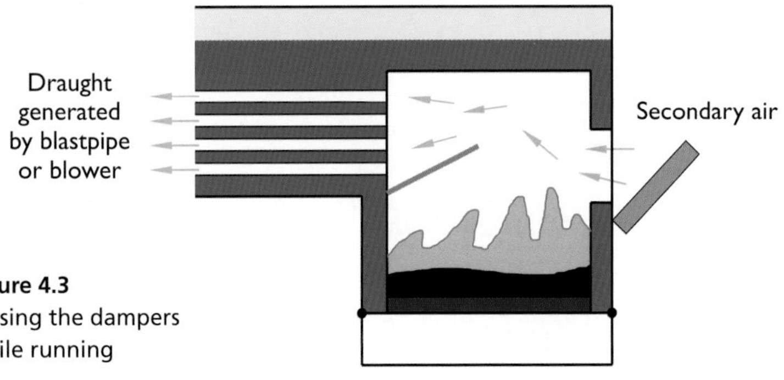

Figure 4.3
Closing the dampers while running

through gaps between the firebars, and this air is referred to as *primary air*. The arrangement is illustrated in **Figure 4.1**. When the locomotive is working, the steam from the exhaust creates a vacuum, which draws gases along the tubes from the fire. To replace these gases more air is drawn into the firebox through the gaps between the firebars. A by-product of the combustion process, ash, falls through the gaps between the firebars. To contain this ash – and also any burning cinders – a tray is fitted underneath the grate. This is called the ashpan, and fitted to the sides of it are flaps, called dampers. The dampers can be used to restrict the flow of primary air, and they are additionally necessary to provide access for emptying the ashpan.

When the locomotive is working, the air flow can be regulated by the fireman in two ways.

First, the dampers can be controlled by rods from the footplate. The dampers are normally open when running, but are often closed during station stops and when coasting to reduce the draught through the fire and help to prevent the locomotive from generating too much steam.

Secondly, the firedoor can be opened slightly when the engine is working, as shown in **Figure 4.2**. This allows air to be drawn into the firebox through the firedoor, and this is known as *secondary air*. Secondary air can be used to reduce the presence of black smoke by completing the combustion of the gases from the fire. However, the more secondary air that is provided, the more air is drawn over the fire rather than through it, which can reduce the effectiveness of the fire.

If a locomotive is steaming very freely the dampers can be closed and the firedoor opened, to allow more air over the fire and less through it, as shown in **Figure 4.3**. This will reduce the rate at which steam is produced.

However, note that on some locomotives excessive amounts of secondary air should be avoided as the cold air can stress the internal surfaces of the boiler when it is hot.

If the locomotive is steaming poorly the dampers can be opened and the firedoors closed, to encourage more air through the fire and less over it, as shown previously in Figure 4.1. This will generally increase the rate at which steam is produced. However, if excessive amounts of coal are added to the fire at one time, black smoke can result.

When a locomotive is working hard and then the regulator is shut off, the draught on the fire (due to the blastpipe) is removed in an instant. If the firedoor is open at this time, there is the risk of a 'blowback' where flames will be emitted from the firedoor onto the footplate in search of air, taking an easier route than along the tubes, as shown in **Figure 4.4**.

Blowbacks can be prevented in a number of ways, depending on the condition of the locomotive. If the regulator is to be shut off for just a moment, for example during a short station stop or a temporary speed restriction during a long climb, then the crew will first turn on the blower to ensure that a draught is retained, thus continuing to draw the flames towards the smokebox. In this circumstance the firedoor may remain open, as a draught is still being provided. If the regulator is to be closed for a long time, for example when approaching a terminus station, the fireman may stop firing well in advance, so that the firebed will be well burned through and not be in search of air. In any case, if there is any worry of a blowback, the simplest approach is to turn on the blower and/or keep the firedoor shut. With the blower on, the fire can be gradually eased down at the crew's discretion.

Note that a blowback will also result from adding large amounts of coal during a station stop unless the blower is turned on. Thus if the firebed needs to be built up during a station stop it is necessary to open the blower accordingly. However, it is quite feasible to add a shovelful or two without the blower, for example to top up a low spot in the fire,

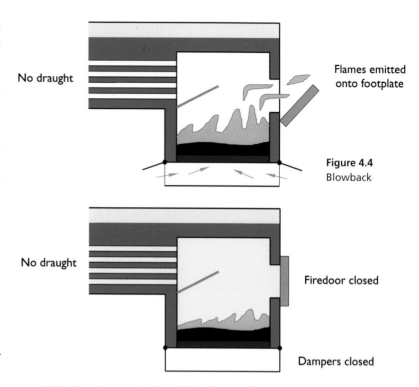

No draught

Flames emitted onto footplate

Figure 4.4
Blowback

No draught

Firedoor closed

Dampers closed

Figure 4.5
Restricting the air flow

provided that the remainder of the fire is calm and consists of coal that is well burned through.

During long station stops or layover periods the locomotive can be left with the damper and firedoor both closed. This will restrict air from getting to the fire, as shown in **Figure 4.5**, and the fire will simply burn through very slowly, keeping the boiler warm.

The general rule for firing a conventional coal-fired locomotive is to 'fire little and often, and fire to the bright spots'. Firing little and often minimises black smoke at the chimney, whilst a bright spot indicates a part of the fire which is thinner than the rest (thus allowing more primary air through).

The appearance of a coal fire when there is no forced draught is shown in **Figure 4.6**. By

Figure 4.6
This view through the firehole shows the appearance of a coal fire when there is little or no draught. In this state it is easy to identify any low spots, such as those to the right of the fire.

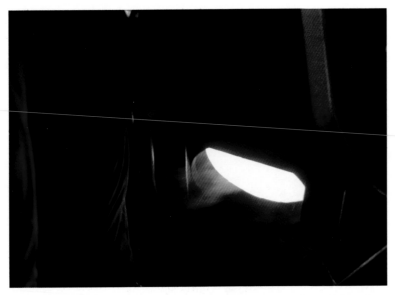

Figure 4.7
With a strong draught the fire burns so brightly that it is virtually impossible to identify any high or low spots. Here the fireman is preparing to fire the next shovelful of coal.

comparison, the appearance of a coal fire when there is a substantial forced draught is shown in **Figure 4.7**.

It is difficult to identify the thickness of a fire when the locomotive is working hard, so there are a few methods which can be used if the fireman is unfamiliar with a particular locomotive:

1. Become familiar with the size of the firebox when the engine is stationary, by adding a shovelful or two of coal. This will determine how many shovelfuls will be required to cover the grate when the locomotive is working.

1. Remember where each shovelful of coal is directed, so as to ensure that the whole grate is fed with coal as appropriate.

1. For locomotives with steeply sloping grates, ensure that the higher part of the grate receives more coal than the lower part. The extra coal will get shaken down the grate by the motion of the locomotive.

1. Use station stops to check the fire for thickness and evenness. Corrective action can be taken during the station stop if necessary or by remembering the condition of the fire when next firing on the run.

1. If it becomes necessary to check the fire when the locomotive is working, open the firedoor and briefly use the end of the shovel, overturned, to deflect the secondary air; this will reveal any low spots.

To get the best out of different types of coal may require different firing techniques to be adopted. Some coals give off heat more quickly than others, depending on their chemical content. Moreover, some coals are more prone to stick together in large lumps, a characteristic called 'caking', which restricts the flow of primary air. Some coals have higher ash content and are more prone to create clinkers, these being solidified lumps generated by molten ash. These lumps cannot fall into the ashpan and hence they restrict the flow of primary air. Therefore, the fireman learns the best way to fire a particular type of coal through experiment and practice.

During the operating day the performance of the locomotive will gradually become impaired if the condition of the fire deteriorates, for example if there is a large build-up of ash or clinker. Although the fireman cannot stop this from happening, a key skill is the ability to determine whether the condition of the fire is such that it requires cleaning, and to determine an appropriate method for doing so.

Further details regarding the lighting up, cleaning and disposal of a coal fire are provided in later chapters.

Gas Producer Combustion System (GPCS)

The conventional coal fire in a steam locomotive may be maintained as a thin bed or built up to be very deep. Most often the fire is kept as a thin bed, as shown in **Figure 4.8**. The draught generated by the blastpipe or blower pulls the primary air through the fire from the ashpan when the firedoor is closed. The greater the amount of air that is pulled through the fire, the hotter the fire becomes. With this thin fire the combustion process is completed close to the fire, and any secondary air drawn in through an open firedoor will simply act to cool the gases from the fire on their way through the firebox and the boiler. Thus, when keeping the fire thin, crews learn to keep the firedoor closed as much as possible so as to avoid this cooling effect. With a thin fire the exhaust gases tend to remain clean, provided that only a small amount of coal is added each time. A by-product of the coal is ash, and with a thin fire this ash can easily drop straight through the gaps in the grate and into the ashpan.

The disadvantage of the thin fire is that it can only provide a limited amount of heat. If more coal is added on top of the thin fire, thus building it into a deep fire, then more heat can be provided. This is because the gases from the bottom part of the fire, for which combustion is complete, now react in a different way with the coal on top. The result is the production of gas rather than heat from the top part of the fire. This gas then requires secondary air to complete its combustion, as shown in **Figure 4.9**, otherwise smoke will be generated. The combustion of these gases above the fire produces more heat than would be provided by the thin fire alone. To summarise, the result of building a deep fire is to produce more heat and thus to generate more steam in the boiler. This is why it is common to find firemen building up the fire before steep climbs, because they quickly learn that more steam can be generated this way.

Unfortunately there is a major disadvantage in building a deep fire. The ash produced by the coal at the top of the deep fire now has to descend through the hot part of the fire to fall into the ashpan. When heated by the hot base of the fire, this ash turns molten and then solidifies as clinker. Therefore, after a short length of time a deep fire can become clogged up with large lumps of clinker at the bottom, which tend to prevent the primary combustion air from being drawn through the fire. Most firemen soon discover that, whilst they can generate more steam by building a deep fire, the benefits are only provided for a limited time, until clinker has formed at the base of the fire. However, when top-quality coal with non-clinkering properties is used, a deep fire may be maintained almost indefinitely.

There have been numerous attempts by locomotive engineers to optimise the combustion process within the space limitations of the locomotive firebox. The aim has often been to achieve high combustion rates, by using a deep fire indefinitely with mediocre-quality coal and without generating clinker. The first system to be widely successful in achieving this aim is known as the Gas Producer Combustion System (GPCS).

The GPCS has two key features. These are a supply of steam to the ashpan and an increased intake of secondary air above the fire, even when the firedoor is closed. The arrangement is illustrated in **Figure 4.10**.

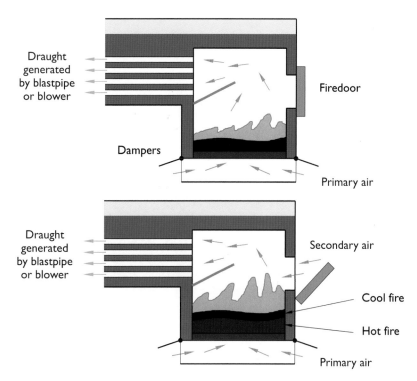

Figure 4.8 Thin fire

Figure 4.9 Deep fire

Figure 4.10 Gas Producer firebox

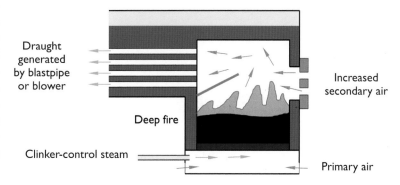

The steam supplied to the ashpan is drawn up through the fire along with the primary air. It cools the bottom of the fire, stopping it from turning the ash into clinker, and is therefore known as clinker-control steam. Simultaneously, as this steam is drawn up through the fire it reacts with the coal to produce combustible gases instead of heat. Thus, by the time all the chemical reactions have taken place between the steam, the primary air and the coal, from the bottom of the fire to the top, there is a large amount of combustible gas generated at the surface of the fire.

The increased intake of secondary air above the fire completes the combustion of all the gases and in doing so produces a vast amount of heat. Hence, the GPCS effectively generates the heat of a deep fire whilst maintaining the bottom of the fire in a cool state that will not form any clinker.

The clinker-control steam is usually a small portion of the locomotive's exhaust steam, piped from the blastpipe to the ashpan and distributed under the firebars, as seen in **Figure 4.11**. In this way, the harder the locomotive works, the more clinker control steam will be provided, so the whole process is automatic. A small portion of steam from the blower valve is also piped to the ashpan. This ensures that clinker control continues when the locomotive is raising steam whilst stationary. For different types of coal the amount of clinker control steam has to be set accordingly. Sometimes the adjustment of this steam supply is carried out on shed by engineering staff; sometimes it is placed under the control of the crew.

The dampers are usually set up to provide a fixed amount of primary air to be taken into the ashpan with the clinker control steam. The dampers have much less effect on the control of a deep fire than with the conventional thin fire, but they usually remain fitted and provide a useful access to the ashpan.

In large locomotives fitted with the GPCS the secondary air is drawn in through special tubes through the side of the firebox. On smaller locomotives it is sometimes possible to draw all the required secondary air in through special ports in the firedoor, as shown in **Figure 4.12**. In either case these tubes or ports are sometimes fitted with vanes to encourage the air flow to become turbulent. This turbulent flow of air in the firebox is beneficial in throwing coal particles out of the rising gas flow. This keeps fine coal particles within the firebox until they are fully combusted.

The GPCS is proven to be more effective in burning the gases that are produced by the coal, which also gives a clean exhaust from the chimney whenever the locomotive is working. The general procedure for lighting up and operating a GPCS-fitted locomotive is essentially the same as for a conventional coal-fired locomotive, the only major difference being the requirement to run with a deep fire. Thus, the fireman of a GPCS-fitted locomotive will have to build up a deep fire at the start of the day whilst making as little smoke as possible, and must then keep the fire deep by firing little and often. The deep fire is generally easier to manage than a thin fire, but has one drawback. The fireman will need to become familiar with the quality of the coal being used in order to determine how quickly the bottom of the deep fire is turning to ash. Such a build-up of ash at the bottom of the fire will hinder steaming if it is not attended to by an appropriate fire-cleaning technique.

Cleaning a coal fire

The coal fire in a steam locomotive produces by-products such as ash and clinker. The amount of ash generated depends mainly on the quality of the coal, whilst the amount of clinker generated is partly dependent on the

method of firing. The fireman tries to keep the generation of clinker to a minimum, but it is difficult to avoid completely.

When large amounts of ash and clinker are formed they will adversely affect the heat developed by the fire and thus have a negative impact on the performance of the locomotive. This can be corrected by using fire irons, as illustrated in **Figure 4.13**, to clean the fire bed. However, the cleaning of the fire tends to result in coal being wasted in two ways. Firstly, partially burnt coal particles can end up being removed with the ash and clinker. Secondly, more coal is required to rebuild the fire ready for the locomotive's next duty.

If it is possible to operate the locomotive all day without cleaning the fire, the fireman will do so. However if the coal is unfamiliar, the fireman will normally choose appropriate times when the locomotive is standing, typically during layover periods, to examine the fire for ash and clinker, and then take the appropriate course of action.

Figure 4.13
Typical fire irons

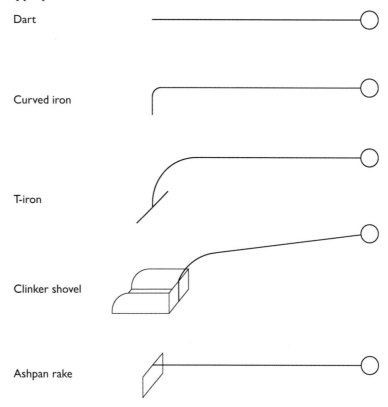

Dart

Curved iron

T-iron

Clinker shovel

Ashpan rake

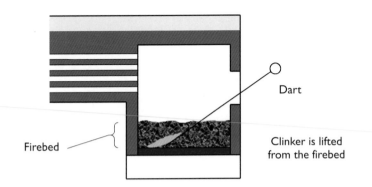

Figure 4.14
Using the dart to find clinker

The function of the different types of fire iron is as follows:

The *dart* has two common functions. It can be poked through the fire to break up coal that has caked together in big lumps. It can also be used to search for clinker, by pushing the pointed end down to the firebars and lifting the bottom of the fire, as shown in **Figure 4.14**.

Locomotives fitted with the GPCS do not generate clinker, provided that they are functioning correctly and are fired appropriately. However, the coal will still produce ash, which needs to be removed by cleaning the fire bed. Here the fireman of a GPCS locomotive has to develop an extra skill. As the GPCS fire is very thick, the fireman has to judge the extent of the ash build-up at the bottom of the fire. This is achieved through experience and by perception of when the steam generation of the locomotive boiler starts to falter.

The frequency with which the fire will need cleaning, and the extent of the cleaning, will depend on many factors. These include the characteristics of the locomotive (*e.g.* size of the grate), the quality of the coal, and how hard the locomotive is being worked. These factors also determine what type of fire irons will be carried on the locomotive.

The fire irons are generally only used when the locomotive is standing or is coasting down a long gradient, when the demand on the fire is at a minimum. As with the skill of firing on the run, the skill of cleaning the fire is learned best by experiment and practice.

A *curved iron* is ideal for manipulating the fire to remove ash and clinker. It can be used in at least two ways. It can be used to move the good fire to one side so that ash and clinker can be easily accessed. Alternatively, it can be used to knock ash through to the ashpan without disturbing the good fire on top. This is achieved by pushing the end of the fire iron down to the firebars and then pushing it backwards and forwards along the bars. This latter method is particularly helpful when cleaning a thick fire, as shown in **Figure 4.15**.

The *T-iron* has basically the same function as the curved iron, but as shown in Figure 4.13 it has a curved stem. This allows the fireman to clean the fire directly under the firedoor at the rear of the firebox, which would be inaccessible using a straight fire iron.

A *clinker shovel* is used to collect clinker and any other waste products that are too large to be pushed through the gaps between the firebars. The large debris is then removed through the firedoor. The clinker shovel can also be used during the preparation of a locomotive, to remove the cold waste products from the grate before preparing to light a new fire.

The *ashpan rake* is used to withdraw ash from the ashpan. It is particularly important on locomotives with small,

Figure 4.15
Using the curved iron to remove ash

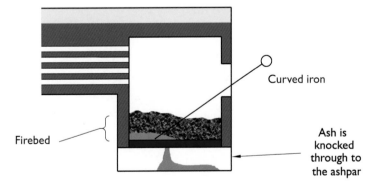

flat-bottomed ashpans, which can quickly become clogged with ash during fire cleaning.

A locomotive will not carry all the fire irons listed above, only those appropriate to the locomotive's characteristics, the quality of the coal and the work the locomotive is carrying out. However, most locomotive sheds possess extra fire irons that can be used by the crew when preparing and disposing of the locomotive.

Locomotives with a basic fixed grate tend to require a greater array of fire irons for cleaning the fire. Therefore, to remove the need to use many of the fire irons, more modern designs of locomotive include extra features to assist handling of the fire, and these are described below.

The *drop grate* has some or all of its firebars mounted on a pivot. When operated via suitable handles and linkages, the drop portion of the grate can be opened like a door in the grate, allowing large clinkers and by-products to be pushed into the ashpan, as shown in **Figure 4.16**. The drop grate can eliminate the need for a clinker shovel. Note that the good part of the fire has to be moved to one side before operating the drop grate, or this will also be lost to the ashpan.

A *rocking grate* has its firebars mounted on pivots. When operated via suitable

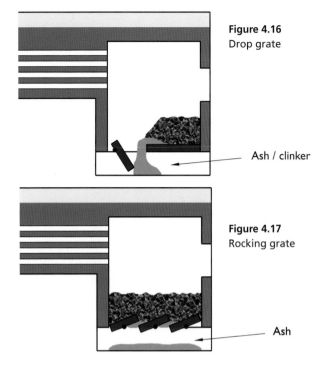

Figure 4.16
Drop grate

Ash / clinker

Figure 4.17
Rocking grate

Ash

handles and linkages, the rocking grate effectively shakes the ash from the bottom of the fire into the ashpan, as shown in **Figure 4.17**.

Figures 4.18 and 4.19 show the movement of a rocking grate, which removes the need for cleaning the fire of ash with the curved iron. Most rocking grates are arranged so that the firebars can be selectively rocked through a full 90°, for disposing of large clinkers and by-products in the same way as the drop grate.

Figures 4.18 and 4.19
Inside the firebox of locomotive Oliver Cromwell the rocking grate is clearly seen. Figure 4.18 shows the firebars when level, whilst Figure 4.19 shows them when rocked.

Figure 4.20
Hopper ashpan

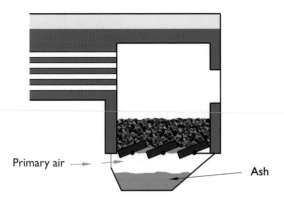

A *hopper ashpan* is typically used in conjunction with the rocking grate. The ashpan is formed as a large hopper with a bottom door. The hopper shape ensures that ash falls right to the bottom of the ashpan, leaving clear space under the firebars for the primary air to enter the firebox, as shown in **Figure 4.20**. Hopper ashpans usually have a large capacity, so they can hold large amounts of ash until the locomotive can be positioned over an ash pit, and the bottom door opened to allow the ash to fall out. The hopper ashpan eliminates the need for the ashpan rake, and allows for much cleaner disposal of ash from the locomotive.

Cleaning the smokebox and tubes

When the locomotive is working the boiler tubes collect soot and the smokebox collects ash and char, which are by-products of the combustion of the fire. The presence of soot in excessive quantity hinders the heat transfer through the tubes to the water in the boiler, and thus reduces the steam-generating capability of the boiler. Therefore, the smokebox has a door on the front, to allow access for cleaning the tubes and the smokebox. This cleaning is carried out on shed using a long rod with bristles around the end, as shown in **Figure 4.21**. The rod is pushed and pulled along each of the tubes to scour away the soot into either the smokebox or the firebox (and hence the ashpan).

If there are large flues present, fitted with a superheater as described in a later chapter, these flues cannot be cleaned with the long rod, so it is common to use a steam or air lance to blast any deposits from them.

Whilst the locomotive is in steam and working, it is possible to clean the tubes by sprinkling sand into the firebox. The gases from the fire then convey the sand along the tubes to the smokebox, scouring the soot away.

Coal-fired locomotives tend to throw burning cinders from the fire out of the chimney. On hot dry days this can cause lineside fires. To overcome this nuisance, many locomotives are fitted with spark-arrestor equipment in their smokebox. This comes in a variety of forms, the most basic being the box-type spark-arrestor, shown in **Figure 4.22**. This system consists of a mesh

Figure 4.21
Cleaning the tubes

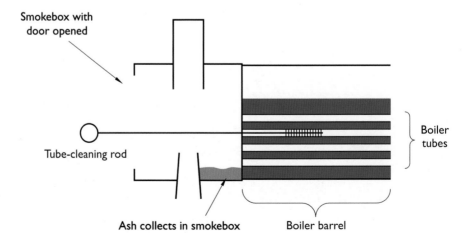

screen which completely surrounds the blastpipe and chimney inside the smokebox. Thus it stops large cinders from passing through it to the chimney, whilst small cinders are stopped from burning when they collide with the wires of the mesh.

A more advanced form of spark-arrestor is the self-cleaning type, shown in **Figure 4.23**. In this system the cinders collide with a baffle plate at the back of the smokebox. They are then drawn by the draught around a passage formed in the bottom of the smokebox, and around the sides of the blastpipe. Finally, the cinders pass through a mesh screen in the front of the smokebox before being ejected from the chimney. As with the box-type spark-arrestor, large cinders are prevented from passing through the mesh to the chimney, whilst small cinders are stopped from burning when they collide with the baffle plate and the wires of the mesh screen.

Access to the mesh screen of a self-cleaning spark-arrestor is achieved by opening the smokebox door, as shown in **Figure 4.24**. Note that the mesh

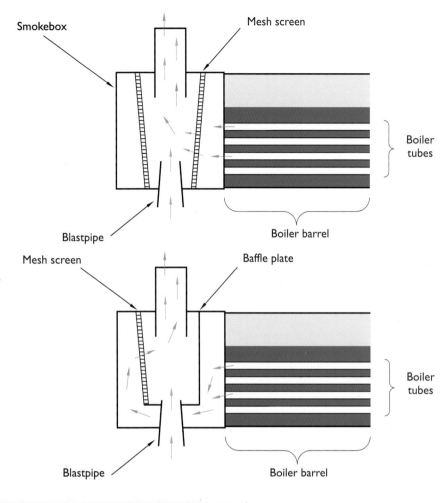

Figure 4.22
Box-type spark-arrestor

Figure 4.23
Self-cleaning spark-arrestor

Figure 4.24
Inside the smokebox of locomotive Oliver Cromwell is a self-cleaning spark-arrestor. In this view the fine-mesh screens are seen in position in front of the chimney base. Also seen is the method by which the smokebox door is tightly secured shut by means of the central dart and the vertical bar.

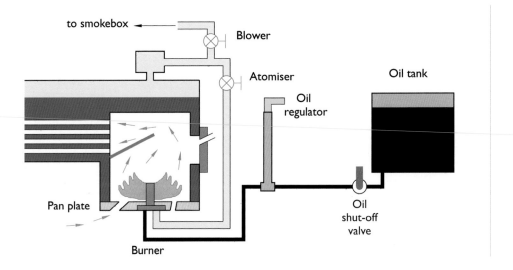

Figure 4.25
Basic oil-firing
equipment

Figure 4.26
This view through the
firedoor shows an oil
burner surrounded by
the air intake tubes of
the pan plate. When
turned on, the
atomiser steam sprays
oil out of the burner
annularly, and
combustion is
completed when the
oil vapour meets the
air sucked in through
the intake tubes.

screens of spark-arrestors can become gradually clogged with particles, which need to be brushed off during locomotive preparation and maintenance, or the free steaming of the boiler will be hindered.

Oil firing

A common alternative fuel for steam locomotives is fuel oil. It is primarily adopted by railways wanting to reduce the spark-throwing of their locomotives and eliminate the risk of starting lineside fires. Oil firing also provides the fireman with greater control of the output from the boiler, and reduces the time required to prepare and dispose of the locomotive.

There are slight variations in the range of equipment that can be installed on oil-fired locomotives. The following description details the oil-firing system that has been widely used by the Welsh narrow-gauge railways. It can be easily fitted to any coal-fired steam locomotive by the replacement of a few components and fitting appropriate pipework. The arrangement is illustrated in **Figure 4.25**.

Oil flows by gravity, from an oil tank placed in the locomotive's former coal bunker, through a regulating valve and directly to the burner. However, the oil cannot be burned directly, as it is too thick. Therefore, pressurised steam is taken from the boiler and supplied to the burner, where it sprays the oil into the firebox as a fine vapour. Hence, the control for this steam supply is known as the atomiser.

Air for combustion is drawn in to the firebox through tubes in a specially-designed pan plate, as shown in **Figure 4.26**. This pan plate is fitted to the bottom of the firebox in place of the ashpan of coal-fired locomotives.

The firedoor is fixed shut during normal operation, and only opened for inspection purposes. When lighting the burner, a lit rag is pushed down a small chute, which is built in to the firedoor, and this chute can also be used by the fireman to view the flame.

During normal operation the fireman turns up the oil and atomiser setting as the driver opens the regulator, and turns down these

Figure 4.27
The fireman's side of the cab of an oil-fired locomotive on the Welsh Highland Railway. The oil-regulating handle is at the bottom of the picture, next to the gauge glass. The small green wheel near the side window controls the atomiser steam to the burner, and this is indicated by the pressure gauge to the top right of the photo. At the opposite end of this pipework, the valve with the wooden handle is the blower control.

settings when the driver closes the regulator. The exact amount by which to turn up the settings is determined by watching the colour of the smoke from the chimney. Too much oil generates black smoke; too little leaves the exhaust very clear, and the locomotive may not steam well. The fireman will try to adopt the cleanest possible setting whilst ensuring that the locomotive produces enough steam to carry out its work. The controls of an oil-fired locomotive are seen in **Figure 4.27**.

There is no need with oil-fired locomotives to carry out any fire-cleaning, and locomotive performance is therefore more predictable than that of coal-fired locomotives. However, the oil used in steam locomotives can vary considerably in quality and in its properties. Thicker oils will require the fireman to open the oil-control valve by a greater amount than with thin oils. Different properties of oil may respond best to different atomiser settings, so the fireman must quickly adapt and find the best settings for any given oil.

When lighting up a cold locomotive there is no steam available for the atomiser. Therefore an auxiliary air supply can be

connected to oil-burning locomotives, as shown in **Figure 4.28**.

When the auxiliary air supply is being used the steam manifold is isolated from the boiler using the manifold shut-off valve. The air supply is connected to the manifold and the compressed air is used for the blower and atomiser. The burner can then be lit. Once the locomotive has generated sufficient steam pressure the burner is turned off, and the air supply disconnected. The manifold shut-off

Oil shut-off valve

Figure 4.28
Air supply for lighting up

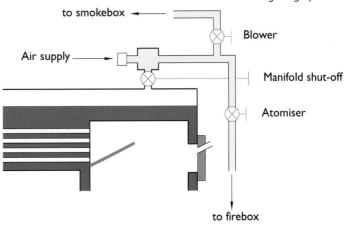

to smokebox

Air supply

Blower

Manifold shut-off

Atomiser

to firebox

Figure 4.29
Oil-system refinements

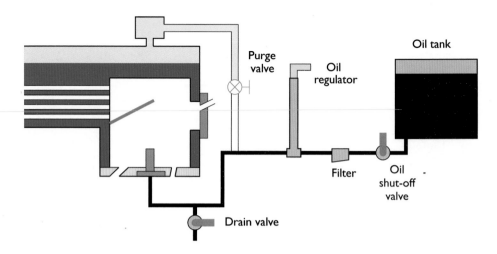

valve can then be opened and the burner relit using steam for the blower and atomiser.

There are further refinements in the oil-burning system, which are used when disposing of the locomotive. The main oil pipe is fitted with a shut-off valve, which will prevent oil leaking if the oil regulator is not properly closed or is worn. In addition there is a drain valve at the lowest point to prevent oil from settling in the burner and clogging up the small passages in the burner. To assist in preventing this clogging many oil-burning locomotives are fitted with a purge valve, as shown in **Figure 4.29**. This valve allows steam from the boiler into the main oil pipe and is used when the burner has been turned off and the oil shut-off valve closed. The steam from the boiler is thus used to flush out from the pipes any remaining oil that might clog the burner if not removed.

A filter is fitted to the main oil pipe to prevent any large particles present in the oil from flowing into the burner. This filter should be cleaned every day.

The flame generated by the oil-burner is intense, so the bottom of the firebox is protected by a ring of firebricks. These firebricks retain heat, making them extremely useful should the burner be accidentally put out whilst running. In such instances the fireman can quickly turn up the oil and it will usually relight straight away using this residual heat from the firebricks. However, the fireman must not wait too long for the burner to relight, as the presence of excessive oil vapour in the firebox can quickly lead to an explosion.

Further details of the procedure used for lighting up and shutting down an oil-burner are provided in Chapters 13 and 15.

Chassis

Chapter 5

Mainframe and suspension

Underneath almost every steam locomotive is a rigid frame. The cylinders are bolted to this rigid frame, whilst the driving wheels, their axles and axleboxes can move up and down in between guides, known as horn guides. The weight of the locomotive is supported on springs, which are typically leaf springs, as shown in **Figure 5.1**.

Spring hanger links are sometimes provided to cater for the change in shape of the leaf spring as it deflects, the bottom of the hanger link being connected to the locomotive's frame. To accommodate the axle and axleboxes the frame has to be cut away, which would be a severe weakness except for the provision of horn stays. These are bars bolted across the frame underneath the axleboxes, and in addition to strengthening the frames they also ensure that the axleboxes, axles and wheels are

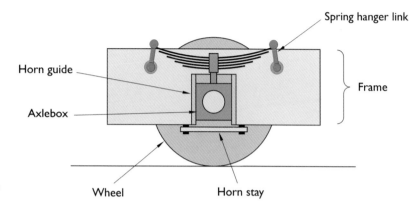

all retained within the locomotive's frame in the event of a derailment. The horn stays have therefore to be removed if it is necessary to change an axle or wheels. **Figure 5.2** shows a typical axlebox arrangement.

The horn guides are sliding surfaces that will wear over time. When they are worn they must be replaced, although some locomotives

Figure 5.1
Horn guides and leaf spring

Figure 5.2
Horn guides and leaf springs are seen most clearly on the tenders of steam locomotives, as in this photograph. The suspension of the locomotive itself is essentially the same but is less obvious because the frames are often between the wheels.

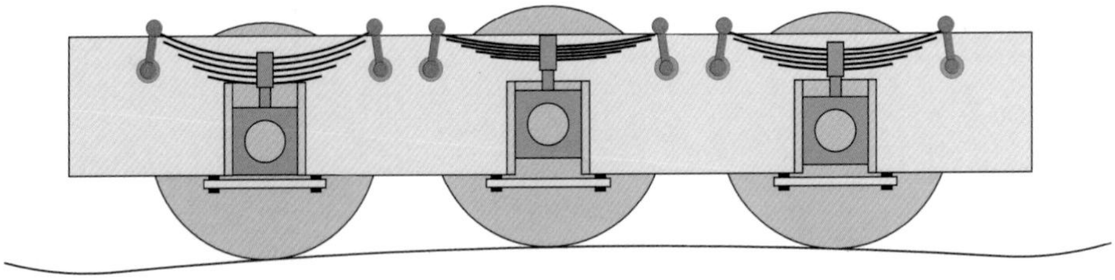

Figure 5.3
Springs accomodating track irregularities

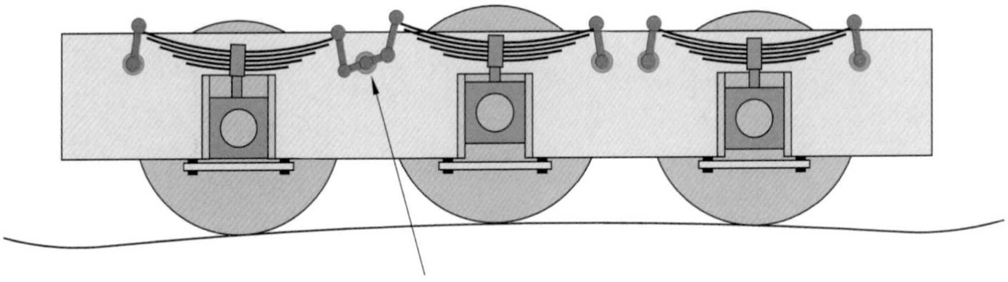

Figure 5.4
Equalised springs

Rocking beam

are arranged with wedges that can be adjusted to take up the wear in the horn guides, thus prolonging the time between overhauls.

The springs allow the locomotive to travel over irregularities in the track without any of the wheels lifting off the rails, as shown in **Figure 5.3**. They also provide a smoother ride for the locomotive crew and crucially soften the impact of the locomotive's weight on the track when there are irregularities.

On locomotives designed for use on very rough track the suspension systems are often refined to include 'equalised springs'. This equalisation is provided by rocking beams between adjacent springs, and a basic form of this is shown in **Figure 5.4**. The rocking beam rotates to accommodate the irregularities in the track, thus taking the strain off the springs,

which then purely act to soften any jolts. Equalising provides a more even loading on each axle.

Driving wheels and coupled wheels

The horn guides prevent the axleboxes from moving back and forth in the frame, and therefore react against the thrusts from the cylinders, which are arranged as shown in **Figure 5.5**.

The connecting rod conveys the thrusts from the pistons to the main driving wheels, whilst coupling rods convey the piston thrusts to the other driving wheels, which are known as the 'coupled wheels', as shown in **Figure 5.6**.

Figure 5.5
Basic frame with driving wheels

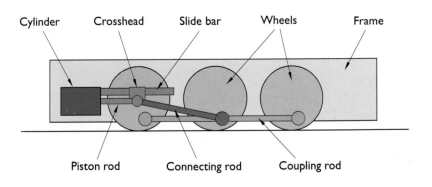

Cylinder   Crosshead   Slide bar   Wheels   Frame

Piston rod   Connecting rod   Coupling rod

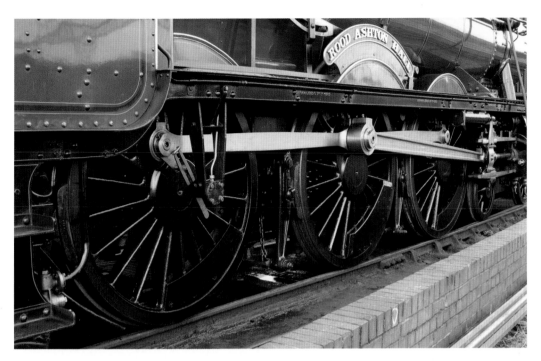

Figure 5.6
This photo shows the connecting rods and coupling rods that transfer the linear thrusts from the pistons to circular motion at the wheels.

For the system to work there must be a connecting rod and coupling rods on both sides of the locomotive, and they must be offset from one another as explained in Chapter 7. Hence the minimum number of cylinders that a locomotive can have is two.

The maximum number of cylinders is usually four, owing to space limitations. There are usually only two sets of coupling rods, one set on each side of the locomotive, regardless of the number of cylinders. The cylinders may be mounted on the outside of the locomotive's frames or between them, and locomotives with three or four cylinders will have two outside the frames and the remainder in between.

It has been shown that the driving and coupled wheels have to be restrained in the frame by the horn guides. The distance between the centres of the foremost and rearmost constrained wheels is called the 'rigid wheelbase' of a locomotive. The more driving wheels that are fitted, and the larger the diameter of the driving wheels, the longer the rigid wheelbase. Unfortunately, the longer the rigid wheelbase, the more difficulty is encountered when travelling around sharp curves, as illustrated in **Figure 5.7**.

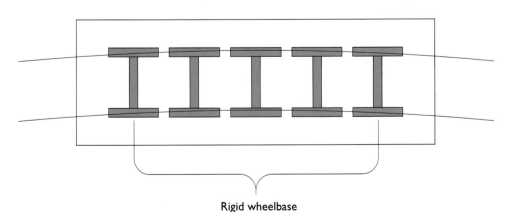

Rigid wheelbase

Figure 5.7
Plan view of long rigid wheelbase on sharp curve

It is often desirable to have the longest wheelbase possible. Freight locomotives are generally fitted with the maximum possible number of driving wheels to maximise the grip on the steel rails. High-speed passenger locomotives tend to need large-diameter driving wheels, because the rotational speed of the wheels is limited by the speed with which the cylinders can operate.

Articulated Locomotives

Articulated locomotives have been devised to overcome problems with the length of rigid-wheelbase locomotives, especially where sharp curves are encountered. Essentially an articulated locomotive is two locomotives in one. Instead of having one long rigid wheelbase the articulated locomotive has two rigid wheelbases, known as power bogies, which are supplied with steam from one large boiler. To enable these locomotives to travel around sharp curves, the power bogies are connected to a mainframe via pivots, as shown in **Figure 5.8**. It is the mainframe that typically carries the boiler, water tank and fuel.

To carry the steam to and from each power bogie articulated locomotives are fitted with a flexible portion to their steam pipes.

There are many different types of articulated locomotive, including the Double Fairlie, Meyer, Kitson-Meyer, Garratt (later Beyer-Garratt) and Mallet. Perhaps the most significant is the Garratt, as shown in **Figure 5.9**. This particular type of articulated locomotive was highly successful at hauling very heavy trains round sharp curves and up steep gradients in places such as South Africa. It is slightly different from other forms of articulated locomotive in having a short mainframe supporting only the boiler. The water tank and fuel bunker are carried on the front and rear power units, which protrude fore and aft of the mainframe.

The Garratt type of locomotive has a very large-diameter boiler and a very large, deep firebox, as shown in **Figure 5.10**. This is the ideal form of boiler for maximum steam generation. The minor disadvantage of the Garratt is that the weight on the driving and coupled wheels becomes uneven as the water and fuel are used.

Figure 5.8
Basic articulated locomotive

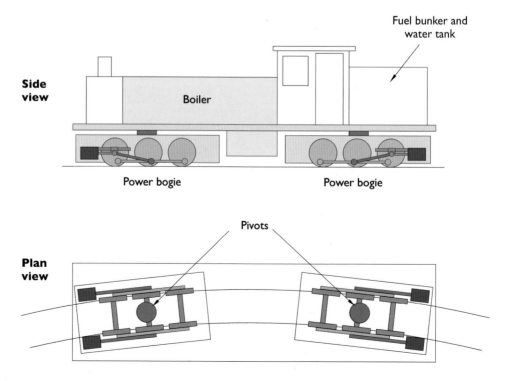

Fuel bunker and water tank

Side view

Boiler

Power bogie   Power bogie

Pivots

Plan view

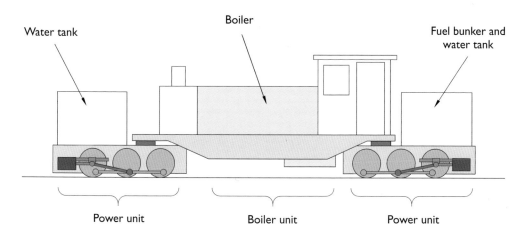

Water tank

Boiler

Fuel bunker and
water tank

Power unit

Boiler unit

Power unit

Figure 5.9
Garratt articulated
locomotive

Carrying wheels

Whether or not a locomotive is articulated, reducing the length of the rigid wheelbase tends to make the locomotive prone to oscillate from side to side as it travels along the track. This phenomenon is known as 'hunting'. In extreme cases this hunting can make a locomotive unstable at high speeds, possibly leading to derailment. Thus, a short rigid wheelbase permits the locomotive to travel through sharp curves but reduces the maximum speed at which it can safely operate. Fortunately the problem is easily overcome by

Figure 5.10
The world's first Garratt articulated locomotive, No K1, seen at Rhyd Ddu, on the Welsh Highland Railway. The Garratt layout allows this 2ft-gauge locomotive to have a very large boiler, with a firebox that is wider than on most standard-gauge locomotives.

Figure 5.11
Frame with leading
and trailing
carrying wheels

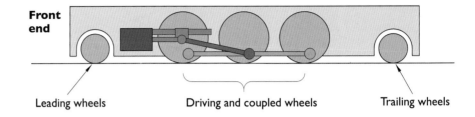

**Front
end**

Leading wheels   Driving and coupled wheels   Trailing wheels

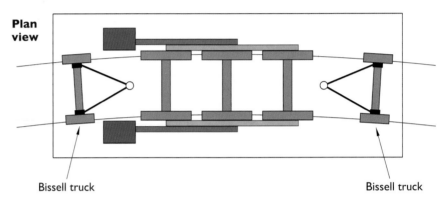

**Plan
view**

Bissell truck   Bissell truck

means of carrying wheels, which can pivot in relation to the frame, as shown in **Figure 5.11**.

The fact that the carrying wheels pivot (in plan view) makes it possible to travel around sharp curves. However, they can also be used to prevent hunting by fitting side springs and friction surfaces. If the right amount of springing and friction resistance is provided, then the locomotive will be both stable at high speeds on straight track and also able to negotiate sharp curves. If the pivoting of the carrying wheels is too stiff, the locomotive's

Figure 5.12
This former GWR tank
locomotive has carrying
wheels at both the
front and rear, which
provide good stability
when travelling around
curves either forwards
or backwards.

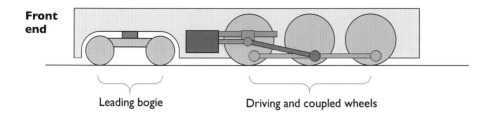

Figure 5.13
Frame with leading bogie and trailing carrying wheels

Leading bogie

Driving and coupled wheels

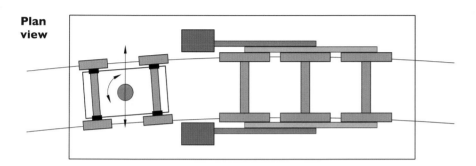

performance on curves will be hindered. If the pivoting of the carrying wheels is too soft, the locomotive's performance at speed will be hindered by hunting.

On a non-articulated locomotive the longer frame with carrying wheels is able to support a larger boiler, as shown in **Figure 5.12**. The carrying wheels also ensure that the increased weight of the locomotive is distributed more evenly on the rails below.

On articulated locomotives it is not always necessary to have carrying wheels because frictional resistance can be provided by the pivot between the mainframe and the power bogies, which has the same function as the springs and frictional resistance of carrying wheels.

There are many different ways of providing carrying wheels. That shown in Figure 5.11 was of Bissell trucks, which have a single axle with an offset pivot point. A similar method is to use Cartazzi axleboxes, which have basically the same function of allowing the carrying wheels to move side to side and rotate to align with the track direction.

Another alternative is a leading or trailing bogie, shown in **Figure 5.13**, which typically accommodates two axles and can both rotate and also slide from side to side under the frame.

As a self-contained short wheelbase the leading or trailing bogie is highly effective at negotiating curves. The bogie's rotational movements can be restricted by friction surfaces which will prevent it from hunting at high speeds. The presence of side springs enables the bogie to steer the locomotive into curves. The exceptional stability of the bogie has made its application popular on high-speed express locomotives, an example being illustrated in **Figure 5.14**.

Figure 5.14
The leading bogie of locomotive Lord Nelson is typical of an express passenger locomotive, providing excellent stability at high speeds and also guiding the locomotive through curves.

Adhesion

Steam locomotives have steel wheels, which run on steel rails. Thus the contact between the wheels and the rails is naturally slippery. However, the grip (or adhesion) can be improved by increasing the weight on the wheels.

Every locomotive is designed to haul a specific weight of train. Heavier trains can be hauled by increasing the weight carried by the locomotive's driving wheels, thus providing better adhesion on the steel rails. However, the amount of weight that can be placed on each wheel is limited by the strength of the track on which it runs. Therefore, locomotives that are required to haul heavy loads are usually given a greater number of driving wheels, in order to spread out their extra weight. The weight of locomotive that is carried by the driving wheels is critical to its haulage capability, so it is commonly referred to as the 'adhesive weight'.

Unfortunately the adhesion obtainable between the wheels and rails is not consistent.

When the rails are wet these surfaces become very slippery and the adhesion is greatly reduced. Thus in wet weather, the locomotive's driving wheels can lose their grip on the steel rails. Sometimes this slipping is only momentary, and it can be countered by closing then reopening the regulator. In conditions where the locomotive continues to slip, the adhesion can be improved by the application of sand between the wheels and the rails.

Gravity sanding, as shown in **Figure 5.15**, is the most basic system for applying sand to improve adhesion. Dry sand is contained in covered sand boxes on the locomotive. Sand flows from the bottom of each sand box down a pipe that is permanently directed at the interface between the driving wheels and the rails. The flow of sand is stopped by a simple shut-off valve, operated by a linkage from a handle in the cab. Thus the sander can be turned on and off by the locomotive crew as required.

Gravity sanding has a number of limitations, mainly due to the very gentle flow of sand under gravity. For example, high winds can blow the sand away from the rails as it leaves the discharge pipe. Also, most heritage railways work their locomotives in both directions, and in wet conditions water can be sprayed up into the discharge pipes by the wheels. The falling sand then becomes wet and sticks in the end of the pipe, and the sanding system becomes ineffective.

Steam sanding, as shown in **Figure 5.16**, attempts to overcome the limitations of gravity sanding by using steam to force the sand along the pipes and then to spray a fine film of sand towards the wheel-rail interface. Dry sand is contained in covered sand boxes on the locomotive, and flows directly into a sand trap. This has an abrupt upwards passage within it which stops the flow of sand under gravity. When sanding of the wheel-rail interface is required, the driver operates a steam valve in the cab, which allows steam from the boiler to travel into the sand ejector. Inside the sand ejector the high-pressure steam is accelerated by a nozzle in the direction of the wheel/rail interface. This ejection of steam

Figure 5.15
Gravity sanding

Figure 5.16
Steam sanding

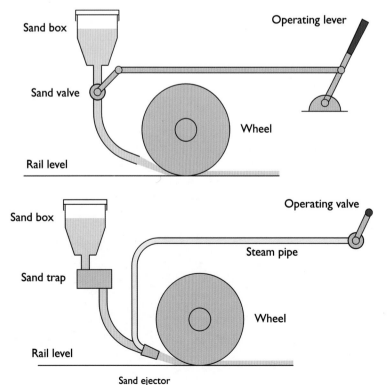

draws the air out of the pipe connecting the sand trap to the ejector, generating a vacuum. Sand is then sucked from the sand trap to the sand ejector and sprayed towards the wheel/rail interface.

Steam sanding can have many refinements, which are designed to maximise their effectiveness and reliability. For example, there are often drains in the steam pipe which allow condensate to drip out when the sander is not in use. This helps to prevent the sand nozzle from clogging up with wet sand. A typical installation is seen in **Figure 5.17**.

Air sanding works in exactly the same way as steam sanding, but instead of using steam from the boiler the sand is ejected by air from the locomotive's main air reservoir. Air sanding would most likely be found on locomotives fitted with air brakes, where an air pump is already present.

Figure 5.17
All the major components of a steam sander are seen in this photograph. These are the sandbox, with sand trap underneath, and the sand ejector.

Chapter 6 | Cylinders

Slide valves and piston valves

The pistons of a steam locomotive push and pull in a linear motion. This motion is converted to rotating motion by the connecting rod and crank. The position of the connecting

Figure 6.1
Slide valve

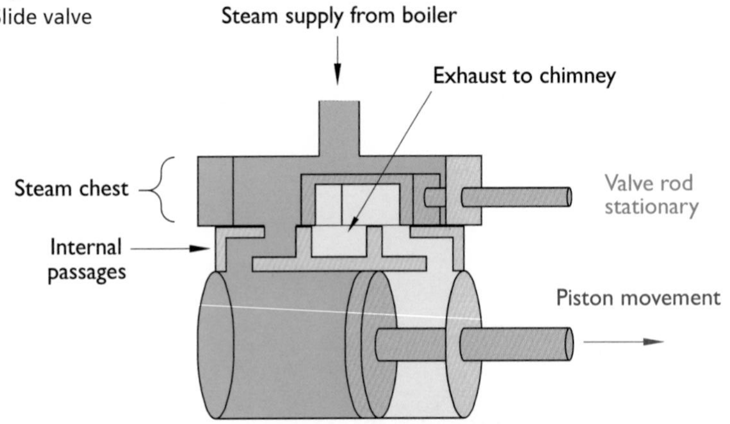

Steam supply from boiler

Exhaust to chimney

Steam chest

Internal passages

Valve rod stationary

Piston movement

rods on each side of the locomotive are offset so that one piston is moving whilst the other is at the end of its stroke.

As the pistons move back and forth in the cylinders, the steam supply from the boiler is controlled so that it alternately pushes on each side of the piston when required. This is often referred to as 'double acting'. To control the steam supply from the boiler to one side of the piston and then to the other, a valve must be used.

There are two common types of valve used for this task on steam locomotives. These are slide valves and piston valves. The slide valve consists of a chamber above the cylinder in which a cup is pushed back and forth, uncovering and connecting internal passages, as shown in **Figure 6.1**. This chamber is commonly referred to as the steam chest. As shown, the steam from the boiler is being diverted to the

Figure 6.2
The cylinder on Tyseley-based ex-GWR locomotive Rood Ashton Hall. The shape of the top of this cylinder reveals that it has piston valves.

50

left-hand end of the piston, pushing it to the right, and any air or used steam on the other side of the piston is routed into the central exhaust passage. This central passage leads to the locomotive's blastpipe and chimney. Note that if the valve were to be moved to the left, it would switch the connections between the passages. The steam from the boiler would be diverted to the right hand of the piston and the steam on the left-hand side of the piston (now used and hence at low pressure) would be routed to the chimney. Thus, moving the valve controls motion of the piston back and forth in order to turn the wheels.

Slide valves have a major disadvantage. The steam from the boiler pushes down on the cup, causing it to wear quickly. To overcome this problem, the piston valve was devised. This arrangement has two piston heads fixed on a piston rod. The pressure of the steam acts only on the ends of the piston heads and does not force them against the sides of the chamber, which in this case is cylindrical. The external appearance of a cylinder with piston valves is highly distinctive, as shown in **Figure 6.2**.

There are two types of piston valve; they are known as outside admission and inside admission.

The outside-admission piston valve is so called because the steam from the boiler (known as live steam) is supplied to the outer ends of

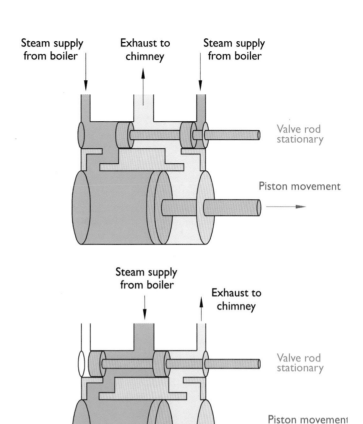

the piston valve heads and the exhaust takes place between them, as shown in **Figure 6.3**.

With the inside-admission piston valve live steam is supplied between the piston-valve heads and the exhaust takes place at the outer ends, as shown in **Figure 6.4**.

The internal passages connecting the valve to the cylinder have to be travelled over by the piston valve heads. Therefore, the openings in the valve chamber are discontinuous, as seen in **Figure 6.5**. This effectively provides bridges to carry the piston valve heads over the passages.

Cylinder and valve events

Using the inside admission piston valve as an example, we will now examine what happens as the cylinder does its work. At the start of the piston stroke, the valve must direct the steam to the end of the cylinder where the

Figure 6.3
Piston valve –
outside admission

Figure 6.4
Piston valve –
inside admission

Figure 6.5
The chamber of a piston valve, the piston heads and rod having been removed. The slotted openings lead into the ends of the cylinder below.

piston is positioned, as shown in **Figure 6.6**. The steam from the boiler now directly pushes on the left-hand side of the piston, pushing it to the right. Note that the port at the other end of the cylinder is connected to the exhaust, so that any used steam on that side of the piston will be easily pushed out.

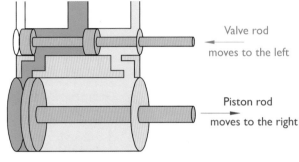

Figure 6.6
Admission of steam

Valve rod
moves to the left

Piston rod
moves to the right

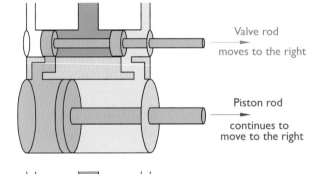

Figure 6.7
Expansion of steam

Valve rod
moves to the right

Piston rod
continues to move to the right

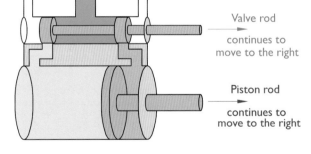

Figure 6.8
Compression

Valve rod
continues to move to the right

Piston rod
continues to move to the right

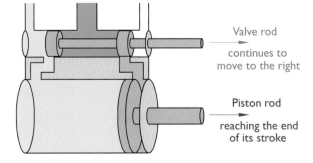

Figure 6.9
Exhaust of steam

Valve rod
continues to move to the right

Piston rod
reaching the end of its stroke

With a locomotive running at slow speed and pulling a heavy load it is desirable that the steam from the boiler will continue to push the piston for most of its stroke. However, when running at speed it is desirable that steam is used more economically. Thus, if the valve now moves to the right it will close the connection between the boiler and the piston, as shown in **Figure 6.7**. This position is known as the cut-off. The steam that is now trapped in the cylinder (on the left-hand side of the piston) is at the same pressure as when it was supplied from the boiler, and will continue to expand and push the piston to the right. However, it will lose its energy more quickly now that the full force of the boiler pressure is no longer behind it.

When the locomotive is travelling at speed the piston moves very rapidly between the ends of the cylinder. The piston head is relatively heavy, so to reduce the force when it reaches the end of its stroke the valve can be moved further to the right. This traps the used steam on the right-hand side of the piston and provides a cushioning effect, as shown in **Figure 6.8**.

As the piston reaches the end of its stroke to the right, the steam on the left-hand side is no longer required, so a further movement of the valve will connect this steam to the exhaust passage, as shown in **Figure 6.9**. If the valve moves by a sufficient amount then steam from the boiler will be directed to the right-hand side of the piston before the end of the piston's stroke, which at high speed will ensure that steam is entering the cylinder ready for the return stroke.

The piston is now ready to repeat the cycle above as it works back towards the left-hand end of the cylinder. The valve will initially continue to move to the right, thus supplying steam from the boiler directly to the right-hand side of the piston as viewed.

Drain cocks

When a steam locomotive has been standing for a length of time any steam that remains in the main steam pipe (which connects the boiler to the cylinders) will cool down and condense back into water. If this water is present when the locomotive starts working again, it will be carried into the cylinders. It has already been shown that part of the cycle of the pistons in the cylinders is compressive, but since water is not compressible like steam, there is a risk that the cylinders, piston rods, etc could be damaged. It is possible, in extreme circumstances, that the force will be large enough to burst off one of the cylinder end covers.

Drain cocks are valves that connect each end of the cylinder to atmosphere at the lowest point, as shown in **Figure 6.10** and visible in Figure 6.2. When opened, these valves allow some of the steam to escape from the cylinders, taking with it any condensate that may be present. When the drain cocks are closed, the steam is totally trapped in the cylinders and will function as shown on the previous pages. The traditional way of opening and closing cylinder drain cocks from the footplate is by a mechanical linkage. However, modern steam locomotives are often fitted with steam-operated drain cocks, to which a valve on the footplate supplies steam from the boiler to close and hold shut the drain cocks. Many locomotives are fitted with an additional drain cock connected to the valve chamber above each cylinder.

Cylinder drain cocks have one other important function. When a locomotive is standing, the presence of any lubricator steam (or steam leaking past the regulator valve) could build up in the cylinders and eventually push the piston, causing the locomotive to make an involuntary movement. This is why it is very important to ensure that the drain cocks are opened before leaving a locomotive.

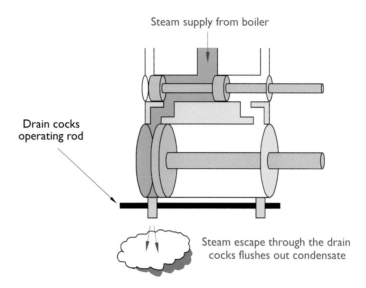

The cylinder drain cocks will allow any such steam to escape straight to atmosphere.

Figure 6.10
Cylinder drain cocks

Drifting

Anti-vacuum valves

When a locomotive is coasting with the steam supply shut off (commonly known as drifting), the pistons are pushed back and forth in the cylinders by the momentum of the locomotive. With no steam present, the cylinders and valves act like an air compressor, sucking air from the main steam pipe and forcing it out through the blastpipe. The resulting vacuum in the main steam pipe provides a resistance to the movement of the pistons, and hence tries to slow the train down. To overcome this problem many locomotives are fitted with anti-vacuum valves, sometimes referred to as snifting valves. This is simply a non-return valve connecting the main steam pipe with the surrounding atmosphere, as shown in **Figure 6.11**.

Figure 6.11
Anti-vacuum valve

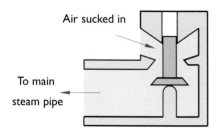

Valve OPEN (locomotive drifting)

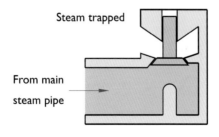

Valve CLOSED (locomotive working)

The anti-vacuum valve allows air to be sucked in to the main steam pipe by the action of the cylinders, preventing a vacuum when the locomotive is drifting. When the regulator is opened and steam is supplied by the boiler the pressure of the steam supply closes the anti-vacuum valve.

The anti-vacuum or snifting valve can be fitted in various places. It is often located above the superheater header on the top of the smokebox. It may also be formed as part of the cylinder.

A disadvantage with the anti-vacuum valve is that cold air is drawn through the cylinders when the locomotive is drifting, and this cools the cylinder walls. When the regulator is eventually reopened there will be a tendency for the incoming steam from the boiler to be condensed when it comes into contact with the cool cylinder walls. This reduces the efficiency of the cylinders, resulting in the use of a greater amount of steam and therefore greater fuel consumption.

By-pass valves

It has been shown that during part of the cycle of the pistons the cylinder is isolated from the main steam pipe, and this can create a vacuum regardless of the presence of anti-vacuum valves. The vacuum can draw dust from the smokebox into the cylinders, where it might score the internal walls. This scoring will result in steam leaks around the sides of the piston, reducing the efficiency of the locomotive, and it is costly to repair.

To overcome this problem some locomotives are fitted with bypass valves. This type of valve is fitted in a pipe which connects each end of the cylinder, as shown in **Figure 6.12**. When the bypass valve is opened any air trapped on one side of the piston can move freely through the connecting pipe to the opposite side of the piston. This greatly reduces the air compression and vacuum generated by the cylinders when the locomotive is drifting.

The by-pass valve is automatic in action. When the regulator is opened steam is taken from the main steam pipe to close the by-pass valve, thus isolating each end of the cylinder. Therefore, when the locomotive is working, the cylinders function as described earlier. When the regulator is closed to shut off the steam supply, the by-pass valve falls away from its seat and the two ends of the cylinder are freely connected.

Note that there are variations in the design of by-pass valves, for example they can also be incorporated into the piston valve heads.

Drifting steam supply

An alternative to the anti-vacuum and by-pass valves is the drifting steam supply. Instead of trying to manipulate the air flow in the cylinders a drifting steam supply provides them with steam even when the locomotive is drifting. This steam supply is just sufficient to keep a positive pressure in the cylinders but not waste too much steam. One of the benefits of using a drifting steam supply is that the cylinders are kept hot, improving their efficiency when the regulator is eventually reopened.

The drifting steam supply is sometimes arranged so that the driver can turn it on and off, and sometimes it is arranged as an excess of lubricating steam, being automatically activated whenever the cylinder drains are closed. The latter makes it imperative that the cylinder drain cocks are opened whenever the locomotive is stationary for any length of time.

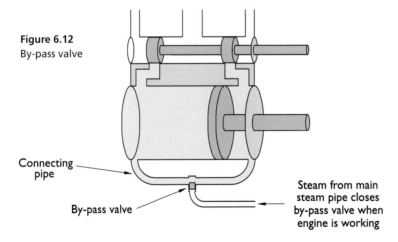

Figure 6.12
By-pass valve

Connecting pipe

By-pass valve

Steam from main steam pipe closes by-pass valve when engine is working

Valve Gear

Chapter 7

Simple valve gear

The previous chapter looked at the function of the cylinders and the valves. However, it will be apparent that there has to be a quick and effective mechanism for controlling the movement of the valve. This mechanism is known as the valve gear.

A simple valve gear is shown in **Figure 7.1**. Both the piston and the valve are each connected to the driving wheels by a connecting rod. The piston uses the main connecting rod to drive the wheels, whilst the wheels drive the valve by the eccentric rod. Note that the eccentric crank is offset from the main crank by 90°.

We will now look at what happens as the locomotive moves forward through one turn of the wheels, starting with the main crank at its lowermost position and the piston central in the cylinder, as shown in **Figure 7.2**. It can be seen that in this position the valve is at its furthest to the left, allowing steam at boiler pressure to enter the cylinder and push the

Figure 7.1
Simple valve gear

Figure 7.2
Backward stroke

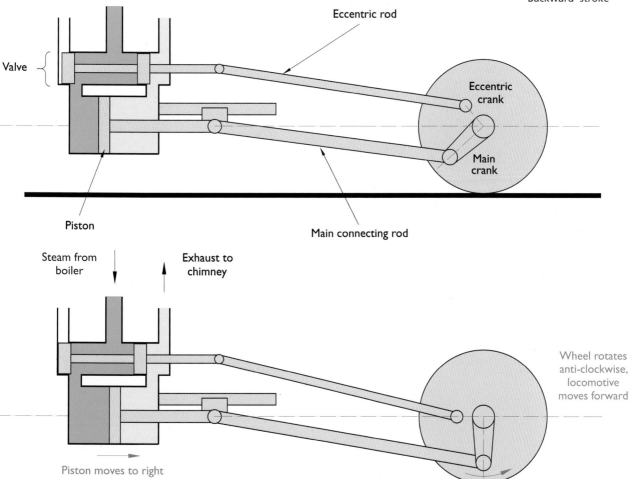

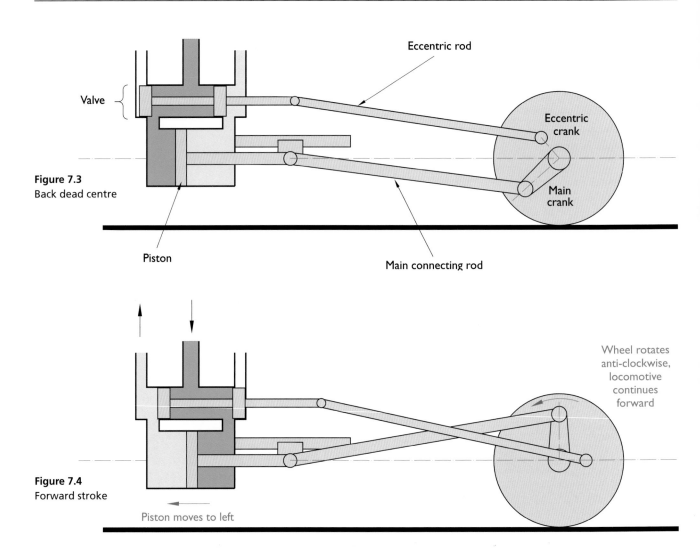

Figure 7.3
Back dead centre

Valve

Eccentric rod

Eccentric crank

Main crank

Piston

Main connecting rod

Figure 7.4
Forward stroke

Wheel rotates anti-clockwise, locomotive continues forward

Piston moves to left

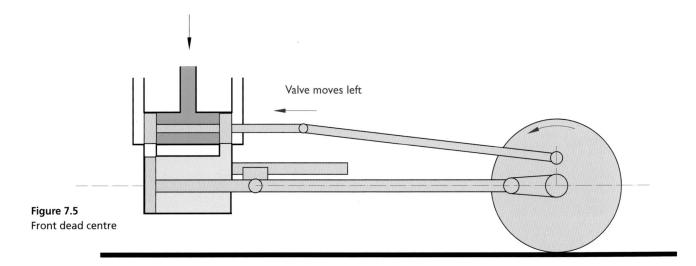

Valve moves left

Figure 7.5
Front dead centre

piston to the right with the maximum possible force. This will turn the driving wheels anti-clockwise as shown and convey the locomotive in the forwards direction, which is to the left. Note that any steam on the right-hand side of the piston (from a previous stroke) is now easily exhausted past the right-hand edge of the valve.

When the piston has reached the end of its backward stroke the valve has moved to its central position, cutting off steam from the boiler to the cylinders, as shown in **Figure 7.3**. This is ideal as the piston cannot do any useful work with the main crank in this position, known as back dead centre. The continued movement of the locomotive in the forwards direction will now be dependent on the other cylinder, which will be at its position of maximum effort.

As the piston begins its return stroke the valve will continue to move to the right and eventually reach its furthest position to the right, as shown in **Figure 7.4**. This directs steam from the boiler to the right-hand side of the piston, pushing it to the left as viewed. The locomotive continues to be moved in the forwards direction.

When the piston has reached the end of its forward stroke the valve has once again moved to its central position, cutting off steam from the boiler to the cylinders, as shown in **Figure 7.5**. The continued movement of the locomotive in the forwards direction will now again be dependent on the other cylinder, which will be at its position of maximum effort.

Introducing lead

The simple valve gear described in the previous section has a severe handicap, due to the eccentric crank's being offset by 90° from the main crank. With this arrangement the steam from the boiler is not admitted to the cylinder until the piston has already started to move, making it less effective when working at high speed. Also steam will be admitted for the duration of the piston stroke – ideal when starting but very uneconomical at high speed. This is because there would be no use of the expansion of the steam contained in the cylinders. To overcome these problems we require the valve to work slightly ahead of the piston movement. The admission of steam from boiler to cylinder in readiness for the piston stroke is known as the lead.

In order to achieve lead (and effectively cut off the steam from the boiler to the cylinders more quickly) we can change the position of the eccentric crank on the simple valve gear so that it is now less than 90° from the main crank. Also note that the piston heads of the valve are manufactured so that they are wider than the passages that connect the valve to the cylinder. This is known as 'valve lap'. The revised arrangement during a backward stroke is shown in **Figure 7.6**. With the piston at its central position the valve has now already started to close. This will soon cut off the steam to the cylinder and thus make use of the expansion of steam trapped in the cylinder.

Figure 7.6
Backward stroke with lead

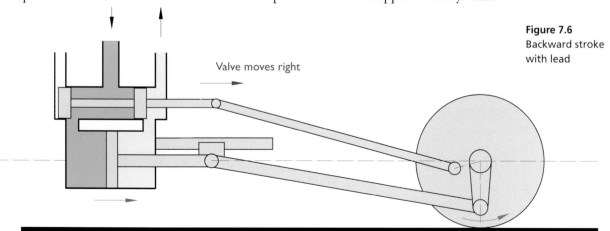

Valve moves right

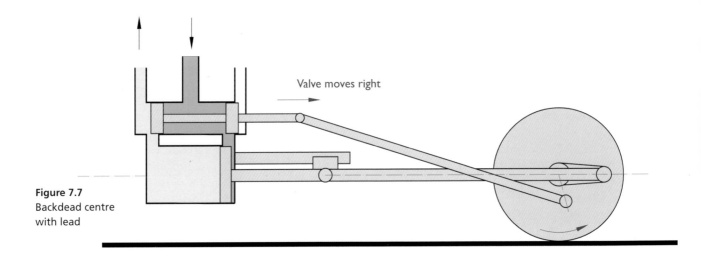

Figure 7.7
Backdead centre
with lead

Valve moves right

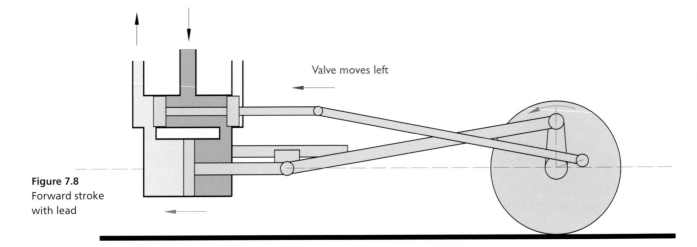

Figure 7.8
Forward stroke
with lead

Valve moves left

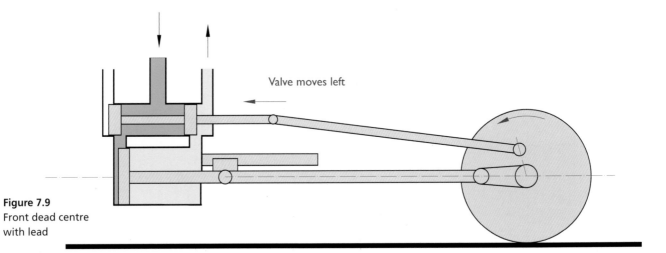

Figure 7.9
Front dead centre
with lead

Valve moves left

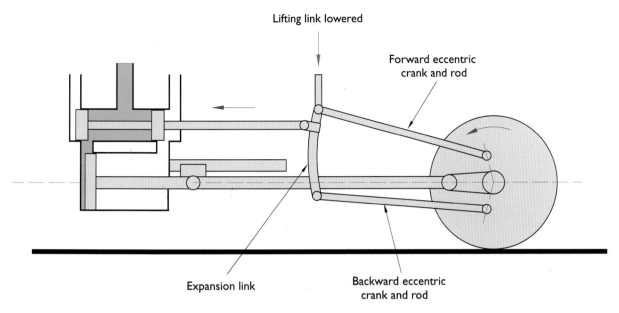

Lifting link lowered

Forward eccentric crank and rod

Expansion link

Backward eccentric crank and rod

Figure 7.10
Stephenson's link motion in forward gear

Before the piston reaches the end of its backward stroke the valve directs steam to the right-hand side of the piston, as shown in **Figure 7.7**. This provides a cushioning effect on the piston and allows time for the steam from the boiler to enter the end of the cylinder in readiness for the forward stroke. The lead also permits an earlier release of the used steam on the left-hand side of the piston, giving it time to exhaust through the passages before the piston returns.

The piston is now immediately subject to the full pressure of steam at the start of the forward stroke, which is shown in **Figure 7.8**. The valve will once again close early in order to provide the cut-off for the forward stroke of the piston.

Before the piston reaches the end of its forward stroke the valve lead directs steam to the left-hand side of the piston, as shown in **Figure 7.9**. This once again provides a cushioning effect on the piston and allows time for the steam from the boiler to move through the passages and enter the end of the cylinder, in readiness for the following backward stroke.

Common valve gear

The simple valve gear with lead would be ideal except that it will only work when the locomotive is travelling in the forward direction. To be fully effective valve gear must be capable of being switched between forward and reverse directions.

We will now take a look at some of the most common types of valve gear that are fitted to steam locomotives, and how they work.

Stephenson's link motion

This type of valve gear works by the same mechanism as the previous simple example. For each cylinder there are two eccentric cranks and two eccentric rods, as shown in **Figure 7.10**. One eccentric crank and rod is arranged for forward gear and the other eccentric crank and rod is arranged for reverse gear. Both eccentric rods are joined by a linkage known as the expansion link, which is supported by a lifting link. This lifting link can be raised and lowered to switch between forward and reverse gear. When it is desired to move the locomotive forwards, the driver places the reverser into the full forward position. This lowers the lifting link so that the eccentric crank and rod arranged for forward running will act directly on the valve, whilst the other eccentric crank and rod will have little effect, as shown in Figure 7.10.

When it is desired to move the locomotive backwards the driver places the reverser into the full reverse position. This raises the lifting link

Figure 7.11
Stephenson's link
motion in reverse gear

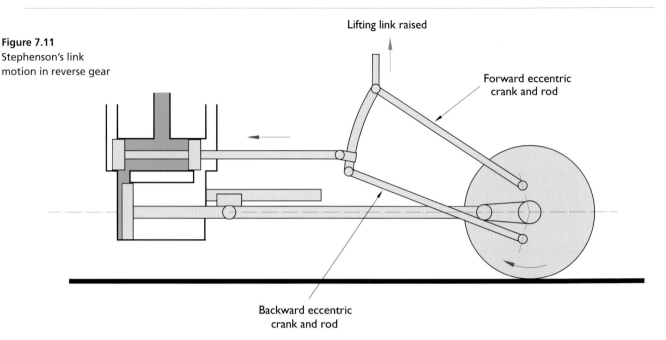

Lifting link raised

Forward eccentric
crank and rod

Backward eccentric
crank and rod

so that the eccentric crank and rod arranged for backward running will act directly on the valve, whilst the other eccentric crank and rod will have little effect, as shown in **Figure 7.11**.

Note that the two Figures 7.10 and 7.11 both show the piston in its front dead-centre position. Therefore, both the forward and reverse rods produce the same valve position, ready to push the piston to the right as viewed.

As the locomotive picks up speed the driver will move the reverser towards mid-gear in order to reduce the amount of steam that is admitted to the cylinders during each stroke. This works by adjusting the lifting link so that the forward/backward eccentric crank and rod will not impart as great a movement to the valve as when the reverser was in full gear.

Note that in the mid-gear position the expansion link will be halfway between the forward and backward eccentric crank and rod. In this position the valve will be moved by a small amount and in complete unison with the piston, whether travelling forwards or in reverse. This movement will allow a small amount of steam from the boiler into the cylinder at the end of each stroke, which will expand during the following stroke to do a small amount of work. Note that running in mid gear is only effective

when the locomotive is already moving with enough momentum to ensure that the forwards or reverse direction of working is retained (*i.e.* the cranks are carried over their dead centres).

Walschaerts valve gear

This type of valve gear is based on the principle that the simple valve gear, with the main crank and a single eccentric crank offset by 90° (as previously shown in Figure 7.1) can be very easily switched between forward and reverse gear. This simplified form of Walschaerts valve gear uses the same eccentric crank and rod to move the valve whether the locomotive is travelling forwards or in reverse. However, the eccentric crank and rod is not directly connected to the valve but to a rocking link, known as the expansion link, as shown in **Figure 7.12**. The rod which moves the valve can be raised and lowered along the expansion link. When it is desired to move the locomotive forwards, the driver places the reverser into the full forward position. This lowers the lifting link so that the eccentric crank and rod will push and pull the rod to the valve in complete unison, as shown in Figure 7.12.

When it is desired to move the locomotive backwards the driver places the reverser into

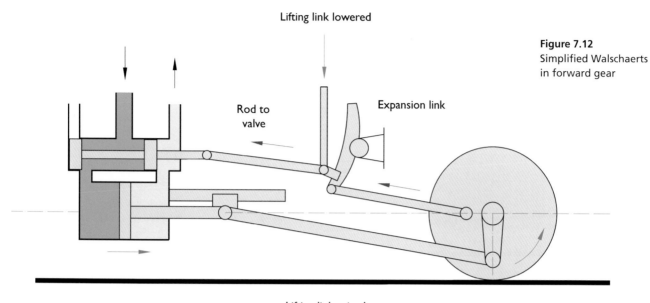

Figure 7.12
Simplified Walschaerts
in forward gear

Lifting link lowered

Rod to valve

Expansion link

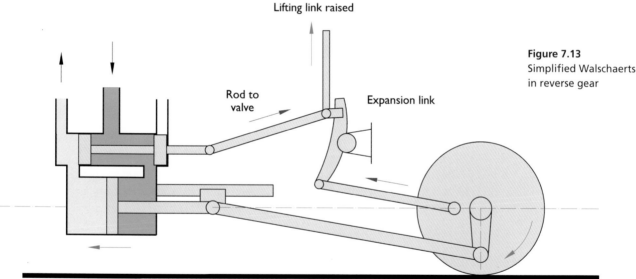

Figure 7.13
Simplified Walschaerts
in reverse gear

Lifting link raised

Rod to valve

Expansion link

the full reverse position. This raises the lifting link so that the eccentric crank and rod will push and pull the rod to the valve in the opposite direction, as shown in **Figure 7.13**.

It will be noticed that in forward and reverse gear the valve has no lead ahead of the piston. Therefore, the piston is unable to work economically and get effective work out of the steam. To overcome this problem the true Walschaerts valve gear is fitted with a link known as the combination lever. This is connected at its lower end to the main piston rod, as shown in **Figure 7.14**. The purpose of

the combination lever is to provide lead by shifting the position of the piston valve, and it works for both forward and reverse directions.

Note that the union link, which is fitted between the combination lever and the piston rod, is simply to accommodate the radial movement of the combination lever relative to the linear movement of the piston rod. The red arrow in the diagram illustrates how the radius rod between the expansion link and the combination lever can be adjusted for forward and reverse gear.

As the locomotive picks up speed the driver

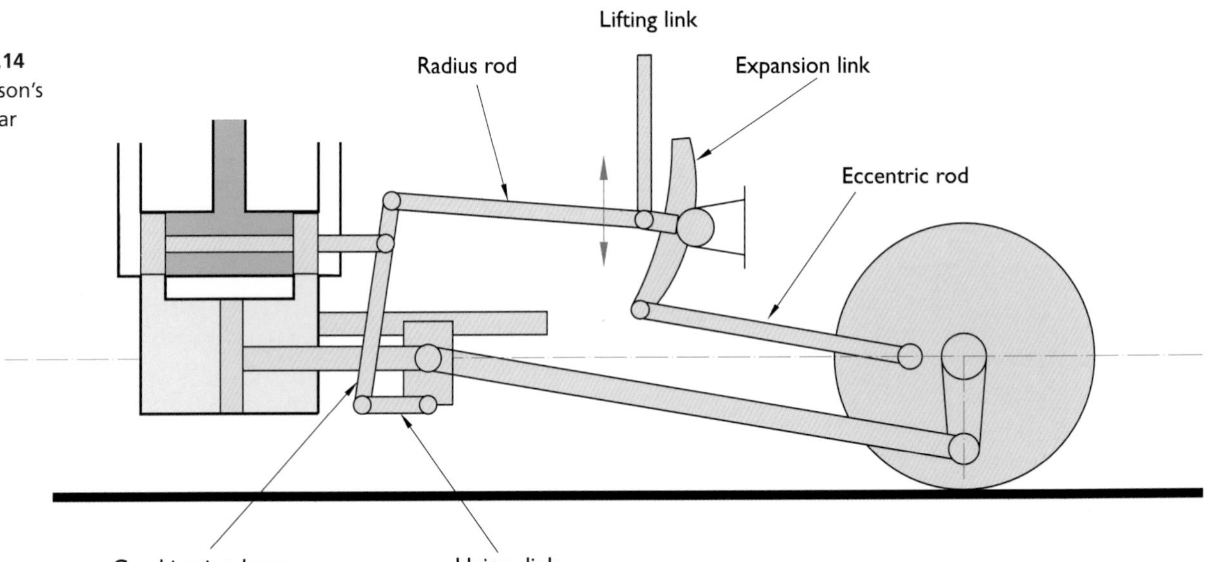

Figure 7.14
Stephenson's
valve gear

Lifting link

Radius rod

Expansion link

Eccentric rod

Combination lever

Union link

will move the reverser towards mid-gear in order to reduce the amount of steam that is admitted to the cylinders during each stroke. This works by adjusting the position of the radius rod in the expansion link, so that the eccentric crank and rod will not impart as great a movement to the valve as when the reverser was in full gear.

Note that in the mid-gear position the radius rod will be at the centre of the expansion link. The expansion link will rock but the radius rod will not be moved at all. Instead, the combination lever will move the valve by a small

amount and in complete unison with the piston, whether travelling forwards or in reverse. This movement will allow a small amount of steam from the boiler into the cylinder at the end of each stroke, which will expand during the following stroke to do a small amount of work.

A typical example of Walschaerts valve gear is shown in **Figure 7.15**.

Hackworth valve gear

This type of valve gear is used on many industrial locomotives, and it functions in exactly the same way as Walschaerts, but is much simpler in its

Figure 7.15
The Walschaerts valve gear is often fitted on the outside of locomotives, where it is easy to access for maintenance purposes. It is possible to locate it outside because it only requires one eccentric rod. The alternative Stephenson's link motion requires two eccentric rods and is therefore usually fitted between the frames, where it is rarely visible to the observer.

construction. The basic Hackworth valve gear has an eccentric crank with no angular offset from the main crank. Instead, the eccentric rod is mounted vertically and moves up and down a slide at its upper end, as shown in **Figure 7.16**. A long rod links the eccentric rod directly to the valve. When it is desired to move the locomotive forwards, the driver places the reverser into the full forward position. This inclines the slide to an angle of approximately 45° so that the vertical movement of the eccentric rod will be converted into a horizontal movement of the rod to the valve, as shown in Figure 7.16. It can be seen that the eccentric crank and rod will not only move vertically, but also horizontally, in complete unison with the movement of the piston. This will impart a direct horizontal movement of the rod to the valve regardless of the position of the slide. The eccentric crank and rod therefore carry out the additional function of the combination lever used in Walschaerts valve gear.

When it is desired to move the locomotive backwards the driver places the reverser into the full reverse position. This inclines the slide to an angle of approximately 45° in the opposite direction to forward gear, so that the vertical movement of the eccentric rod will be converted into a horizontal movement of the rod to the valve, as shown in **Figure 7.17**.

As the locomotive picks up speed the driver

Figure 7.16
Hackworth valve gear in forward gear

Figure 7.17
Hackworth valve gear in reverse gear

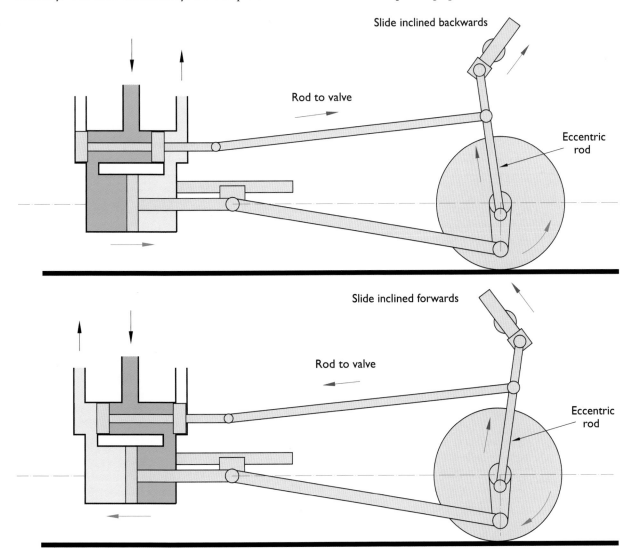

Slide inclined backwards

Rod to valve

Eccentric rod

Slide inclined forwards

Rod to valve

Eccentric rod

Figure 7.18
The minimal parts of the Hackworth valve gear made it popular on industrial locomotives, as shown on this small-scale replica on the Sherwood Forest Railway.

will move the reverser towards mid-gear in order to reduce the amount of steam that is admitted to the cylinders during each stroke. This works by adjusting the angle of the slide, so that the eccentric crank and rod will not impart as great a movement to the valve as when the reverser was in full gear.

Note that in the mid-gear position the slide will be arranged such that the upper end of the eccentric rod will simply move vertically up and down. Therefore, none of the vertical movement of the eccentric rod will be transmitted to the valve. Instead, the horizontal movement of the eccentric rod will move the valve by a small amount and in complete unison with the piston, whether travelling forwards or in reverse. This is exactly the same as the function of the combination lever in Walschaerts valve gear, but is achieved with fewer components.

In full gear the angular movement of the upper end of the eccentric rod acts in exactly the same manner as the eccentric rod on Walschaerts valve gear, providing the main driving movement of the valve.

The Hackworth is one of the simplest forms of locomotive valve gear, using very few parts, as seen in **Figure 7.18**. Unfortunately, it has a major drawback. The vertical positioning of the eccentric rod means that any vertical movement of the locomotive's suspension will impart an undesirable movement to the valve. This can cause jolts when the locomotive is running over irregularities in the track, such as dips and joints.

Alternative types of valve gear

Many different types of valve gear have been used on steam locomotives. They are either variations on the common types previously described, or are radically different because they use poppet valves.

Variations on a theme

There are many variations to the common types of valve gear, although they achieve the same basic objective. The detailed differences are as follows:

- Gooch valve gear and Allan valve gear both function in the same way as the Stephenson's link motion, the only differences being the arrangement of the linkages, and some minor differences in the motion of the valve.
- Joy valve gear and Southern valve gear

function in the same way as the simple Hackworth but are arranged so that suspension movements have much less effect on the valve travel.

- The Baker valve gear combines features similar to both the Walschaerts valve gear and the Hackworth valve gear. It eliminates sliding parts and is largely unaffected by suspension movements.
- The Young valve gear embraces exactly the same principles as the Walschaerts but does not require an eccentric crank and rod. Instead, the required motion is provided by a linkage and rocker shaft connecting with the piston rod on the opposite side of the locomotive (which is 90° out of phase).

Rotary-cam poppet valve gear

This is a radically different form of valve gear. It uses poppet valves to admit steam into the cylinders and to release steam to exhaust. The arrangement of the Caprotti valve gear is illustrated in **Figure 7.19**. Note that the actual arrangement of this valve gear is quite complex, and has therefore been greatly simplified in the illustration.

Above each cylinder is a camshaft with four cams mounted on it. These cams are eccentric to the camshaft, so that as the camshaft is rotated they push down on long rods connected to each

of the poppet valves. In the illustration the cams have pushed open two of the poppet valves, to allow steam from the boiler to enter the left-hand side of the cylinder and to allow steam to exhaust to the chimney from the right-hand side of the cylinder.

The rotation of the camshaft is driven by the rotation of the wheels, via a gearbox mounted on one of the locomotive's driving axles. A torque reaction link is connected between this gearbox and the locomotive's frames, to stop the gearbox from being rotated along with the wheels. The driving shaft from this gearbox is connected to the camshaft via another gearbox, which can alter the angle of the cams. The reversing shaft from the cab is connected to this gearbox, which is used to select between forward and reverse and to adjust the cut-off so as to conserve steam when the locomotive picks up speed.

When the regulator is opened the poppet valves are lifted onto their seats by the pressure of the steam, and forced open as appropriate by the cams on the camshaft. When the regulator is closed, the poppet valves fall from their seats and allow steam to pass freely from one end of the cylinder to the other, acting as by-pass valves when the locomotive is drifting.

Figure 7.19
Caprotti-type rotary-cam poppet valve gear

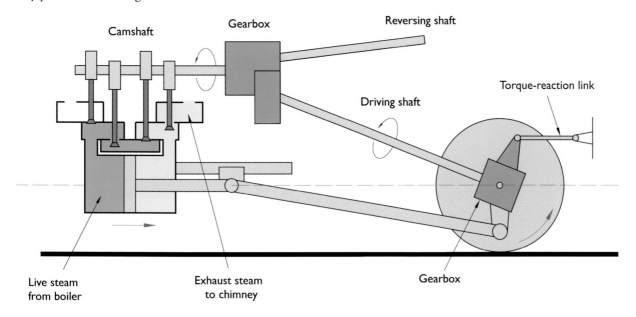

Superheated steam

Steam taken from the boiler directly to the cylinders is defined as saturated steam. When this steam expands in the cylinders it tends to condense and lose its pressure very quickly. The efficiency of steam locomotives can be improved (and hence fuel consumption decreased) by greatly reducing or eliminating the condensation which occurs in the cylinders as the steam expands. This is achieved by raising the temperature of the steam before it reaches the cylinders, a process which is called superheating.

Most large locomotives are fitted with a superheater, as shown in **Figure 8.1**. The main steam pipe leads to a steam chamber inside the smokebox, known as the superheater header. From here the steam is separated into several small steam pipes. Each of these steam pipes then conveys the steam along one of the boiler tubes before returning to the smokebox. Once back in the smokebox the small steam pipes combine in the superheater header. From the

Figure 8.1
Superheating

Figure 8.2
Inside the smokebox of a BR Class 2 locomotive are the superheater elements, which are routed into the large flues. Also visible on each side are the large steam pipes that convey the superheated steam to the cylinders.

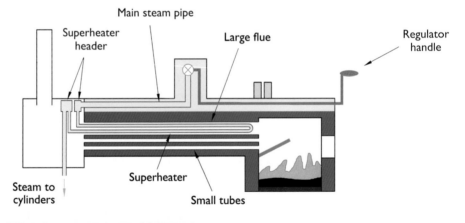

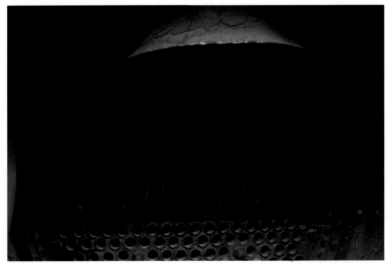

superheater header the steam passes through large pipes to the cylinders.

Note that the superheater header has two chambers, one for steam prior to superheating and one for steam after superheating. However, both chambers are usually part of the same fitting, with a separating wall. Note also that the boiler tubes that accommodate the small steam pipes are larger than the other boiler tubes, and are thus commonly referred to as the large flues. These are clearly seen in **Figure 8.2**.

The passage of gases from the hot fire around the small superheater tubes heats the steam to a higher temperature than it had leaving the top of the boiler via the dome. The

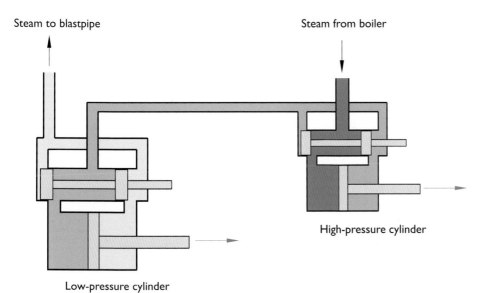

Steam to blastpipe

Steam from boiler

Figure 8.3
Compound
arrangement

High-pressure cylinder

Low-pressure cylinder

superheater tubes are small so as to maximise the area for heat transfer. The actual amount by which the steam temperature is increased is dependent on how many tubes there are in the superheater and how close the superheater tubes reach towards the firebox.

Compound locomotives

A compound locomotive is one in which the steam from the boiler is expanded in more than one cylinder before exhausting to the blastpipe and chimney. The basic arrangement is shown in **Figure 8.3**.

The steam from the boiler is expanded in a small high-pressure cylinder before passing through a pipe to a large low-pressure cylinder. The output force of the high- and low-pressure cylinders is arranged to be the same. The large diameter of the low-pressure cylinder allows it to generate as much force from the partially expanded steam as the high-pressure cylinder extracts from the steam from the boiler.

Although it appears that the steam is being used twice, in actual fact the compound arrangement simply distributes the work of the steam between two cylinders. The difference between the compound arrangement and the conventional simple arrangement (where steam is only expanded once), is that the pressure drop

during each piston stroke is less significant. This reduction in the pressure drop allows the cylinders to work more efficiently, and reduces the strain on mechanical parts of the engine. Compounding is highly advantageous where very high steam pressures are generated by the boiler. The main disadvantage of compounding is that there is typically more equipment than with the conventional simple arrangement. Therefore compound locomotives are more expensive to build and maintain.

There are many variations in compound locomotive design. There may be any number of high-pressure cylinders exhausting into any number of low-pressure cylinders, all made to suitable sizes to extract the energy from the steam in an efficient manner. On rigid-wheelbase locomotives the high-pressure and low-pressure cylinders are usually connected to the same driving wheels, whilst on articulated locomotives the high- and low-pressure cylinders may be used to power different sets of driving wheels. The latter arrangement is seen in **Figure 8.4**.

There are two notable complications with compound locomotives, the first being a difficulty in starting the locomotive, the second a difficulty in achieving an equal distribution of work between the high- and low-pressure cylinders. When starting the locomotive, steam

Figure 8.4
Garratt No K1 was, unusually for its type, a compound locomotive. Steam from the boiler is used first in the rear engine unit (nearest to the camera), then in the front engine unit, before finally being exhausted up the chimney. Note the significantly different diameter of the cylinders on each engine unit.

is allowed from the boiler to the high-pressure cylinders, and it is therefore these cylinders alone that must start the train moving. Once moving, the low-pressure cylinders will begin to assist. This results in the occasional difficulty of starting a heavy train when steam is only available to the small high-pressure cylinders.

To overcome this there are various types of starting devices for compound locomotives. The main two are described below.

The starting valve is fitted to allow a controlled amount of steam from the boiler to by-pass the high-pressure cylinders and hence act directly on the larger low-pressure

Figure 8.5
Starting arrangement

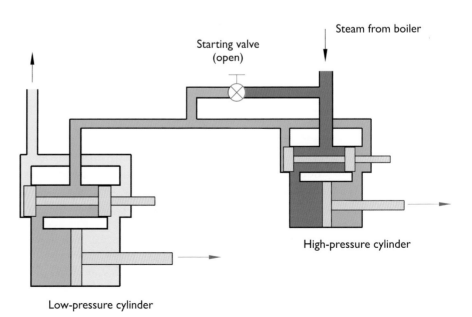

cylinders, as shown in **Figure 8.5**.

The simpling valve goes one step further than the starting valve by allowing the high-pressure cylinders to exhaust directly to the blastpipe and chimney. This permits the locomotive to start by means of simple expansion in all the cylinders, as with a conventional locomotive.

As described in Chapter 7, when a locomotive picks up speed the driver will move the valve gear towards mid-gear. This reduces the amount of steam that is admitted to the cylinders during each stroke and hence utilises the steam more economically. Unfortunately with a compound locomotive this movement of the valve gear will often result in the distribution of work between the high- and low-pressure cylinders becoming uneven. To overcome this difficulty some locomotives are fitted with independent valve gears for the high-pressure and low-pressure cylinders. If this is the case, then the driver will have to learn the required pressure distribution between the cylinders, so that the independent valve gears can be adjusted to provide an even distribution of work between the cylinders.

Compound locomotives were popular in the late 19th century and early 20th century but became less so after the development of superheating. It was found that compound expansion offered much less of an efficiency advantage when used in conjunction with superheated locomotives. Therefore very few compound locomotives survive in working order today.

Exhaust-system refinements

The blastpipe and blast nozzle restrict the escape of exhaust steam from the cylinders. This creates an increase in the steam pressure in the pipes between the cylinders and the exhaust. This pressure is typically referred to as 'back pressure' because it will provide a resistance to the movement of the pistons. Considered another way, the live steam from the boiler has to give up part of its useful energy in forcing the exhaust steam out of the blast

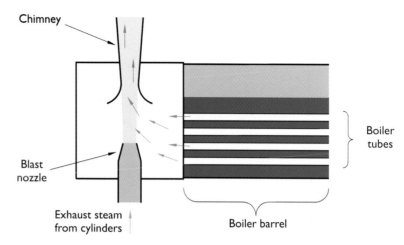

Figure 8.6
Conventional exhaust system

nozzle. In the blast nozzle the exhaust steam is accelerated to high speed, and on leaving the blast nozzle it draws air from the smokebox up the chimney. This creates a vacuum in the smokebox and thus draws air from the firebox end of the boiler, generating a draught on the fire. The traditional arrangement is a single nozzle, as shown in **Figure 8.6**.

The actual size and shape of the blast nozzle and chimney are critical to the performance of the locomotive. The exhaust system should be designed to provide sufficient draught on the fire with the minimum possible amount of back pressure on the cylinders. The importance of an efficient design of exhaust system, i.e. blast nozzle and chimney, is often underestimated.

If the exhaust system is poor it will develop a lot of back pressure. To do the same amount of work at the cylinders this back pressure has to be overcome by supplying an excess of steam from the boiler to the cylinders, which in turn raises the demand on the fire. In order to meet this rise in demand it is common to reduce the size of the blastpipe, thus speeding up the exhaust steam and providing increased draught on the fire. However, this has the disadvantage of further increasing the back pressure on the cylinders and leads to a vicious circle. The end result is either increased coal consumption or the need to use larger locomotives than are really necessary for the work required, both factors increasing running costs.

If it is possible to generate the required

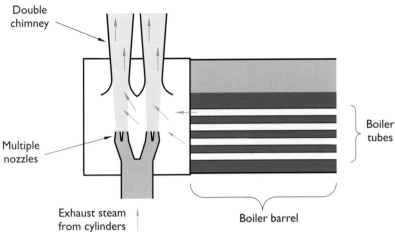

Labels on figure:
Double chimney
Multiple nozzles
Exhaust steam from cylinders
Boiler tubes
Boiler barrel

Figure 8.7
Multiple nozzles and double chimney

draught) can be used to look for further improvements in the exhaust system and hence reduced coal consumption.

It is not surprising that engineers have continually sought to improve steam locomotive exhaust systems, and there have been many different designs. Three of the most notable (all named after their designers) are the Giesl ejector (Dr Adolph Giesl-Gieslingen), the Kylchap exhaust (Kyössti Kyälää and André Chapelon) and the Lempor ejector (Jean Lemaître and Livio Dante Porta).

Improving an exhaust system can be achieved in different ways. One is by obtaining the optimum sizing of the blastpipe and chimney, and the other is by changing the shape and form of these items. Of the latter, two common themes are prevalent. These are using two blastpipes and a double chimney, and/or fitting multiple nozzles to each blastpipe top. The two features are illustrated together in **Figure 8.7**.

draught on the fire whilst having less back pressure, the boiler will not have to supply as much live steam to the cylinders in order to haul the train. This leads to two possibilities: either the locomotive can generate an excess of steam and be used on more strenuous duties, or the reduced steam demand (and hence less required

Lubrication

Chapter 9

Types of lubricant

The steam locomotive incorporates many sliding parts, which will quickly wear out if they are not kept supplied with constant lubrication. There are several different lubricants, of which the most common are listed below.

Thin oil flows easily and is used to lubricate the various parts of the motion including slides and plain bearings, and is also used for the axlebox guides.

Special steam oil can withstand high steam temperatures and has to be used for lubricating the moving parts of the cylinders and valves. However, the steam oil is thick and will not run easily along the pipes to where it is required.

Grease is often used for plain bearings which rotate slowly or simply rock back and forth, and it is also used for all sizes of roller bearing that are fitted on modern steam locomotives.

To supply these different types of lubricant to the parts where they are to be used requires specialised lubrication systems. For each type of lubricant there is often more than one means of supplying it to the sliding parts.

Supplying thin oil

For small plain bearings and guides, for example in the valve gear and the crosshead respectively, it is common for thin oil to be supplied along pipes from oil boxes. If the oil were allowed to flow straight into the pipes to the motion it would run away very quickly rather than providing a controlled gradual

lubrication throughout the train journey. Therefore, the pipes are fitted into the oil box so that the ends are higher than the oil level, as shown in **Figure 9.1**. Between the oil and the pipe ends is a small wire frame with a soft wool material, called a 'trimming'. The oil is siphoned by the wool into the end of each pipe. This is a slow process which provides the control of the oil supply. From the pipe ends, the thin oil drips easily down the pipe under the force of gravity.

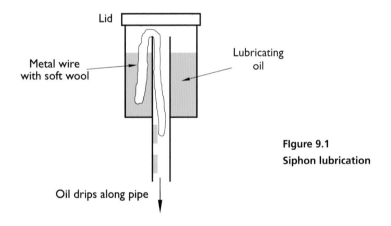

**Figure 9.1
Siphon lubrication**

The level of oil in each oil box is maintained by the locomotive driver throughout the day. However, note that the oil is siphoned all of the time. For this reason the driver will normally not top up the level of the thin oil towards the end of the day, as it will simply leak away during the night.

Sometimes there are shared oil boxes, with several pipes to convey the lubricant to the various locations where it is required. It is also common for there to be dedicated oil boxes, which are located directly above the rotating or rocking bushes that require the lubricant, for example in the coupling rods and the valve gear respectively. **Figure 9.2** shows an example

Figure 9.2
Inside this typical siphon lubrication oil box can be seen the metal wire and soft wool. When in position the soft wool siphons the oil into the pipe, which delivers oil to lubricate the sliding piston rod in the background.

Figure 9.3
Restricted feed

Figure 9.4
Restricted-feed lubrication is commonly found on the coupling rods and connecting rods of steam locomotives. A small reservoir of oil is present under the cork.

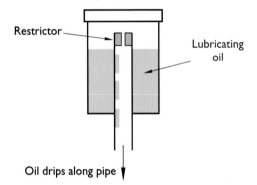

Restrictor

Lubricating oil

Oil drips along pipe

of a dedicated oil box.

There are many variations on the siphon lubrication system. For example, it is possible to have U-shaped pipe ends to siphon the lubricant, rather than the soft wool material. Another example is to have screw-down filler lids, which prevent air entering the oil box, and hence the resulting vacuum restricts the flow of the lubricant.

For plain bearings on the driving rods and valve motion, siphon action is not required, because the parts move rapidly in a circular motion which throws the thin oil all around the oil box, and hence into the ends of the pipes. However, in this case the rate at which oil is supplied is controlled by a restrictor fitted to the end of the oil pipe. This restrictor has a small orifice, as shown in **Figure 9.3**.

Restricted-feed lubrication is often used for the plain bearings of connecting and coupling rods. A small oil chamber is formed in the rod itself, above the bearing, and there is a small refilling hole in the top. When the locomotive is in service, this refilling hole is seen plugged with a cork, as in **Figure 9.4**. Inside the oil reservoir is the raised pipe, as seen in **Figure 9.5**.

The plain bearings that support the weight

Figure 9.5
With the cover removed, the small oil reservoir and restricted passage can be seen.

Figure 9.6
With the axlebox cover opened, the reservoir of oil can be clearly seen. This plain-bearing axlebox is on the tender of a BR Standard locomotive.

of the locomotive on its axles are much larger, and therefore require much more lubricating oil. These plain bearings are located inside the axleboxes and sit on top of the rotating axle. However, the axlebox cannot simply be filled with lubricating oil, because it would easily leak away through the gaps in the side where the axle passes through it. Thus, the thin oil is contained in the bottom of the axlebox, underneath the axle and the bearing, as shown in **Figure 9.6**.

A woollen pad with a tail trimming is kept pressed against the underside of the axle by a steel plate and a spring, as shown in **Figure 9.7**. The tail trimming of the pad hangs down into the oil and soaks it up by capillary action. The woollen pad, when soaked with oil, lubricates the rotating axle.

Note that in addition to the woollen pad a small supply of oil is often fed through small holes in the top of the axlebox and the plain bearing. This small amount of oil is siphoned from separate oil boxes as previously described.

Supplying special steam oil

For lubricating hot sliding surfaces in cylinders and the various steam valves the thick steam oil has to be fed into the steam passages, which are at high pressure. This can

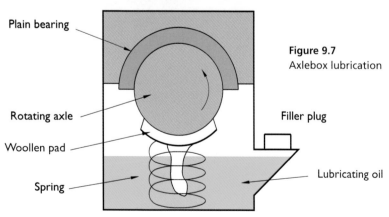

Plain bearing

Rotating axle

Woollen pad

Spring

Figure 9.7
Axlebox lubrication

Filler plug

Lubricating oil

be achieved by either a displacement lubricator or a mechanical lubricator. The displacement lubricator is arranged so that the oil reservoir itself is directly connected to the high-pressure steam pipes when it is in use, and the reservoir of oil is therefore pressurised. Note that only a small quantity of oil is used for lubrication purposes, so, unlike the water ingress caused by priming, the oil does not present any hazard to the cylinders.

The most basic form of displacement lubricator is shown in **Figure 9.8**. When in use the filler plug and drain plug are screwed shut, and the isolating valve is opened. The steam pipe is connected to the displacement lubricator, which is initially full of steam oil. As steam becomes stagnant at the top of the lubricator it condenses into water. The water then sinks to the bottom of the lubricator because its specific gravity is greater than that of the steam oil, which will naturally float on top. As more water collects at the bottom the oil rises until it can flow out of the lubricator and into the steam pipe, where it is carried away with the steam and lubricates the hot surfaces.

Eventually the displacement lubricator will fill up with water as the steam oil becomes displaced into the steam pipe. Therefore it is necessary to drain off the water and refill the lubricator with oil at set intervals. To refill the simple lubricator shown in Figure 9.8 it must be isolated from the high pressure of the steam pipe. This is achieved using the isolating valve, an example being shown in **Figure 9.9**.

The procedure for refilling a simple displacement lubricator is as follows:

1. **Close the isolating valve, to isolate the lubricator from the high pressure of the steam pipe.**

2. **Slowly open the filler and drain plugs, because there may be a small amount of trapped pressure in the lubricator.**

3. **Let the water drain away.**

4. **Screw the drain plug shut.**

5. **Refill the top of the lubricator with steam oil.**

6. **Screw the filler plug shut.**

7. **Open the isolating valve, to restart the lubrication.**

Figure 9.8
Displacement lubricator

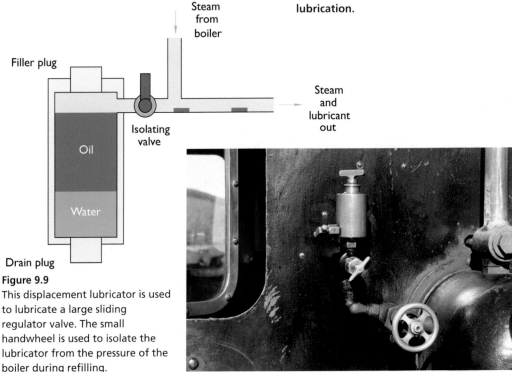

Figure 9.9
This displacement lubricator is used to lubricate a large sliding regulator valve. The small handwheel is used to isolate the lubricator from the pressure of the boiler during refilling.

The sight-feed lubricator, shown in Figure 9.10, is a more sophisticated version of the displacement lubricator. It is typically located in the cab of the locomotive. As with the simple displacement lubricator, the oil reservoir is subjected to the pressure in the steam pipe, when the lubricator is in use. Steam is supplied to the sight-feed lubricator from the boiler solely for the purpose of conveying the lubricating oil to the cylinders and steam valves. The high pressure of the steam from the boiler compared to that present in the cylinders ensures a constant flow of steam through the lubricator. The steam becomes stagnant in two locations, the oil reservoir and the sight-feed glass, where it condenses into water. In the reservoir the oil naturally rises above the water due to its lower specific gravity. From here it is fed through a fine nozzle into the sight-feed glass, which is full of water. Droplets of oil then float up through the water and are displaced into the steam pipe, in the same manner as the basic displacement lubricator. Adjusting the setting of the oil valve gives accurate control over the amount of oil delivered into the steam pipe.

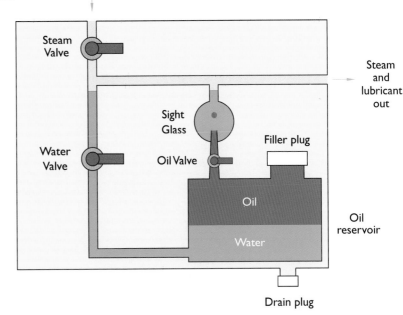

The sight-feed lubricator is shown in **Figure 9.10** with only one sight glass, for reasons of clarity. In reality the reservoir tends to be used to supply multiple sight-feed glasses and hence multiple steam pipes, as seen in **Figure 9.11**. This way one lubricator is used to lubricate several components.

Figure 9.10
Sight-feed lubricator

Figure 9.11
This sight-feed lubricator has multiple sight glasses, each with an oil nozzle inside and each with an associated valve to adjust the oil supply rate.

For the sight-feed lubricator to be refilled it must be isolated from the high pressure. The procedure for refilling such a lubricator is as follows:

1. Close the oil valve, then the water valve, and finally close the steam valve.

2. Slowly open the filler and drain plugs, because there may be a small amount of trapped pressure in the lubricator.

3. Let the water drain away.

4. Screw the drain plug shut.

5. Refill the top of the lubricator with steam oil.

6. Screw the filler plug shut.

7. Open the steam valve and ensure that the sight-feed glasses are full of water. Note that when first starting the lubricator it will take a few minutes for the steam to condense and fill the sight-feed glasses with water.

8. Open the water valve, then the oil valve.

The mechanical lubricator, as shown in **Figure 9.12**, takes oil from an unpressurised reservoir and forces it into the steam pipes. Other than topping up the oil level it requires no control by the locomotive crew. Inside a mechanical lubricator are small cylinders and pistons which pull the steam oil through a non-return valve from the surrounding oil box, and then push it through a non-return valve and along the pipes to the locomotive's cylinders.

The pistons in the mechanical lubricator move very slowly and are driven by a rotating shaft with an eccentric. The rotating shaft is given its rotation by a linkage from the locomotive's motion, as seen in **Figure 9.13**.

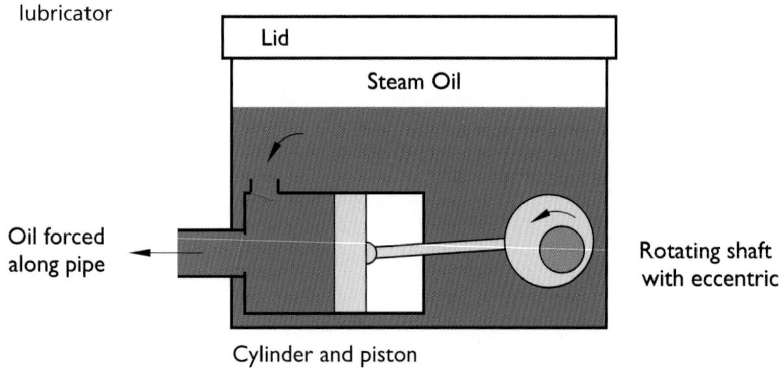

Figure 9.12
Mechanical lubricator

Lid

Steam Oil

Oil forced along pipe

Rotating shaft with eccentric

Cylinder and piston

Figure 9.13
Most mechanical lubricators are positioned on the running plates and are driven by the movement of the locomotive's valve gear.

Therefore the lubrication is automatic whenever the locomotive is moving.

Supplying grease

Grease is very thick, and it is applied by a grease gun to grease nipples on the locomotive. The grease gun forces the grease into passageways leading to the part to be lubricated, as shown in **Figure 9.14** for a rotating part. The grease fills the very small gap around the rotating part, and being thick it will not run away like oil. Only a small amount of new grease is required to replenish that burnt away or forced out by the rotating part. This new grease, when applied at the grease nipple, will simply force along the grease already in the passageway. If grease continues to be applied at the grease nipple it will eventually force grease out of the sides of the bearing surfaces.

Grease lubrication is also used for roller bearings, which are fitted on more modern types of locomotive.

The imperfections that are inherent in sliding surfaces generate friction. This friction resists the relative movement of the sliding surfaces. It has long been understood that an object can be moved much more freely when it is placed on rollers, as shown in the middle of **Figure 9.15**. Unfortunately, the moving object will eventually roll off the end of the rollers, unless each roller is continually

returned from the rear of the moving object to the front.

The roller bearing applies the rolling principle in a circular manner, as shown on the right of Figure 9.15. The rollers are positioned between a rotating shaft and its housing. There is no sliding surface and therefore very little friction. Thus an object mounted on roller bearings will move very freely. To prevent the rollers of a roller bearing from colliding into each other they are separated by a cage structure. This will rub against the rollers, but, as it does not carry the load, wear will be minimal.

Grease is forced into a roller-bearing installation through grease nipples, in the same way as described for the simple rotating bearing. The grease fills the gap between the shaft, rollers, cage and housing.

Unlike simple rotating parts, roller bearings do not usually require daily lubrication by the locomotive crew, the task instead being carried out at set intervals of routine maintenance.

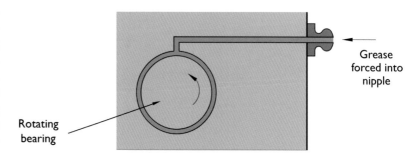

Rotating bearing

Grease forced into nipple

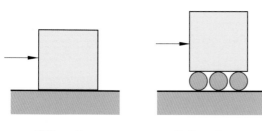

Sliding object   Rolling object

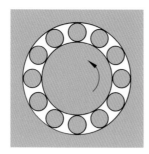

Roller bearing

Figure 9.14
Grease lubrication

Figure 9.15
Roller bearing

Chapter 10

Brakes

Steam locomotives and historic rail vehicles almost always use tread brakes, whereby a brake block is forced onto the outer rim of the wheel. The resulting friction between the brake block and the wheel slows the rotation of the wheel. This decelerates the train. Increasing the force pushing the brake block against the wheel will increase the friction, and hence the deceleration will be more rapid. However, if the force is too great, the wheel could be slowed down too quickly and will instead slide along the rail. Therefore, train braking has to be relatively gentle except in emergency.

Figure 10.1
Tread rake – brakes applied

Figure 10.2
Vehicle equipment

Air brakes

The air brake uses air pressure in a cylinder, pushing against a piston, to provide the force to push the brake block against the wheel, as shown in **Figure 10.1**. The friction generated between the brake block and the wheel will try to move the brake block with the wheel rim. Therefore, every brake block is fitted to a brake hanger link, which prevents the brake block from trying to move round with the wheel.

To begin with, only the locomotive (or its tender) was fitted with brakes. Trains were hauled by the locomotive and stopped by the locomotive. Many historic goods trains are still hauled this way, but with a guard's van at the other end of the train fitted with a handbrake. Thus if one of the couplings were to break, the guard could stop the back portion of the train. However, following serious accidents it became compulsory for all passenger trains to have a fail-safe braking system, whereby all the brakes would be automatically applied if the train were to become separated into two parts. In railway terms these are known as continuous brakes. The air-brake system provides the required fail-safe measure by storing air in an auxiliary reservoir on each vehicle and by controlling it with a triple valve, as shown in **Figure 10.2**. The triple valve is completely automatic in operation, and on modern rolling stock has been superseded by a device known as the distributor, although the function is broadly the same.

Air is supplied by the locomotive along a pipe that is connected between all the vehicles, via flexible end hoses. This is known as the train pipe. The end cocks between vehicles must be opened so that air from the locomotive

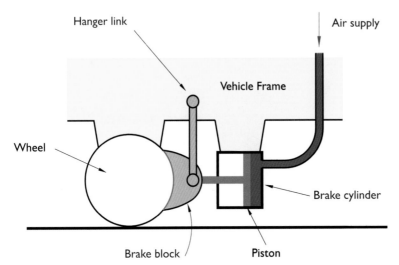

Hanger link

Air supply

Vehicle Frame

Wheel

Brake cylinder

Brake block

Piston

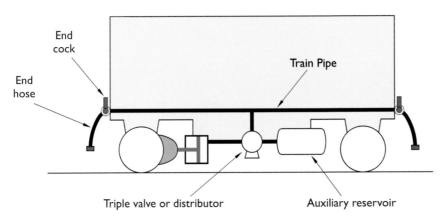

End cock

End hose

Train Pipe

Triple valve or distributor

Auxiliary reservoir

passes all the way down the train. This is verified by momentarily opening the end cock on the last vehicle of the train. If air escapes then it is established that the entire train is being supplied with air. This is known as a continuity test. End cocks have to be fitted so that the last vehicle can be made to retain the air pressure in the brake system. An example of end fittings is seen in **Figure 10.3**. The reason for there being two sets of hoses is explained later.

As the train pipe is charged with air the distributor allows this air to also charge the auxiliary reservoir, but simultaneously empties the brake cylinder of any air pressure. Thus, when the train pipe is full of air, the brakes are released and air is used to fill the auxiliary reservoir, as shown in **Figure 10.4**. In this condition there is no force at the brake blocks, so no braking is taking place. However, as the brake blocks are likely to rub gently against the wheels, causing wear, most brake rigging is fitted with springs that are just sufficient to pull the brake blocks away from the wheel but

not strong enough to counter the braking force. This is not shown on the diagrams, for reasons of clarity.

When the pressure in the train pipe falls, as shown in **Figure 10.5**, the distributor

Figure 10.3
On the buffer-beam of this air-braked locomotive are two end hoses. When not connected to adjacent vehicles the ends of the hoses are hooked onto retaining brackets, to prevent them from being damaged.

Figure 10.4
Vehicle with brakes *released*

Figure 10.5
Vehicle with brakes *applied*

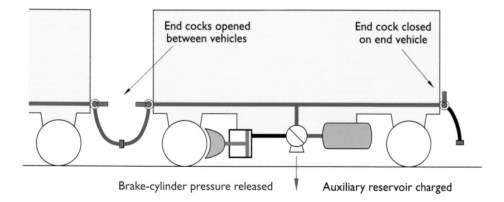

End cocks opened between vehicles | **End cock closed on end vehicle**

Brake-cylinder pressure released | Auxiliary reservoir charged

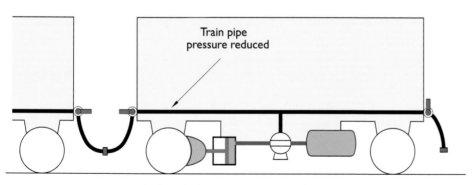

Train pipe pressure reduced

Brake cylinder pressurised by air from auxiliary reservoir

Figure 10.6
The air pump on former Southern Railway locomotive Lord Nelson has been neatly positioned under the cab. Notice the piston rod between the steam and air cylinders.

automatically uses the air previously stored in the auxiliary reservoir to pressurise the brake cylinders and apply the brakes.

- The driver reduces the pressure in the train pipe to apply the brakes.
- The driver increases the pressure in the train pipe to release the brakes.

If a coupling breaks, the end hoses are pulled apart and the air escapes from the train pipe to atmosphere. Hence, the train brakes are all applied in the event of the train becoming separated. However, once stationary the air pressure will very gradually leak away, so the train must be secured by a handbrake or chocks (called 'scotches' in railway terminology) if it is to be left for more than a few minutes.

The distributor effectively controls the severity of the braking in inverse proportion to the train-pipe pressure. In other words, the

more the train-pipe pressure is reduced, the greater the air pressure is increased in the brake cylinder. This is all controlled by the action of the distributor.

The air pressure for operating the brakes has to be generated by the locomotive. This is achieved using a steam-powered air pump, as seen in **Figure 10.6**.

The air pump is powered by steam from the boiler, via a shut-off valve, as shown in **Figure 10.7**. The air compressed by the air pump is stored in a reservoir, which is known as the main air reservoir. From here the air passes through the driver's control valve to the train pipe. The pressure of the air regulated into the train pipe is usually less than that stored in the main reservoir.

The driver's control valve has two functions. It can allow air from the main reservoir to enter the train pipe to release the brakes, as shown in Figure 10.7, and it can let

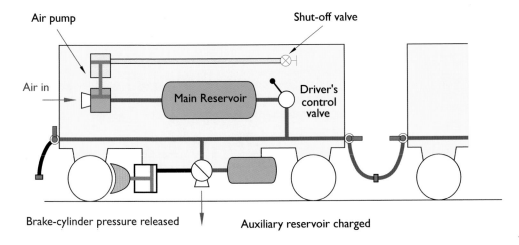

Brake-cylinder pressure released   Auxiliary reservoir charged

Figure 10.7
Locomotive with
brakes *released*

Figure 10.8
Locomotive with
brakes *applied*

Brake cylinder pressurised by air from auxiliary reservoir

Figure 10.9
A typical modern
air-brake controller.
The position of the
handle corresponds to
an associated pressure
in the train pipe.
The handle is moved
to the left to release
the brakes, and to the
right to apply them.

air out of the train pipe into the atmosphere to apply the brakes, as shown in **Figure 10.8**.

A typical modern air-brake controller is seen in **Figure 10.9**. Such controllers have many internal components, and their function provides the driver with fine control over the train-pipe pressure, and hence the severity of the braking. These numerous internal components are the reason for the considerable size of the base of the controller.

The cab of the locomotive is fitted with pressure gauges connected to both the train pipe and main reservoir. From this the driver will know the severity of any brake application and can also verify the reserve of air available for releasing the brakes.

The air-brake system as described above has one major drawback. When a brake application is made, the distributor permits rapid movement of air from the auxiliary reservoir to the brake cylinder. Similarly, when the brakes

are released the distributor permits rapid release of air from the brake cylinder to atmosphere. However, the recharging of the auxiliary reservoirs with air from the train pipe is not so

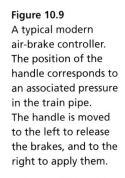

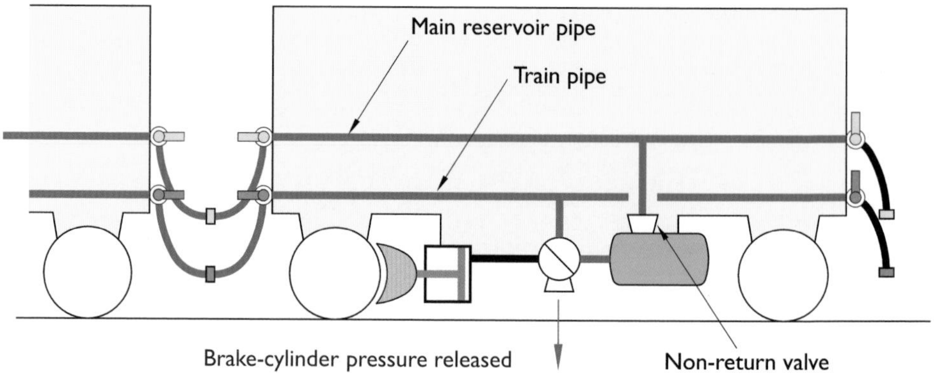

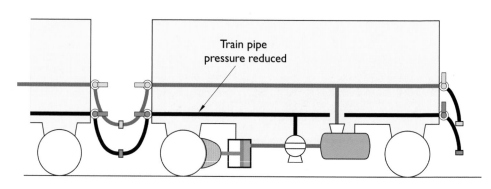

Figure 10.10
Twin-type system with brakes *released*

Figure 10.11
Twin-type system with brakes *applied*

rapid. Thus, if a driver was to make a succession of brake applications, it is possible that the auxiliary reservoirs would not have sufficient time to fully recharge with air. Hence the effectiveness of the brake might be lost.

To reduce this problem the distributors can be fine-tuned to delay the brake release, thus allowing time for the auxiliary reservoirs to recharge. However, to overcome the problem completely, the twin-pipe air system was devised. This system works in exactly the same way as before, but has a second air pipe running along the length of the train, as shown in **Figure 10.10**. This pipe is directly connected to the locomotive's main air reservoir (it does not go through the driver's control valve) and to the auxiliary reservoirs on each vehicle. It is therefore known as the main-reservoir pipe, and it remains charged with air regardless of what the pressure may be in the train pipe.

The function of the main-reservoir pipe is to keep the auxiliary reservoirs topped up with air pressure at all times, even when braking is

taking place, as shown in **Figure 10.11**. This way there will not be a shortage of air even if there is a succession of rapid brake applications and releases. The only exception is if the train becomes separated into two parts. In this case both the train pipe and the main-reservoir pipe will lose their air pressure to atmosphere. However, a non-return valve ensures that the auxiliary reservoir retains whatever air it has stored at that point in time.

To avoid any confusion the end fittings are colour-coded. The standard colour coding is red for the train pipe and yellow for the main-reservoir pipe. It can be seen from the diagrams that, if the end fittings were accidentally crossed over, the main-reservoir pipe would be connected directly to the train-brake pipe. As this is potentially dangerous the end fittings of the main-reservoir pipe are fitted with special valves, which permit air to flow only between main-reservoir-pipe connections and not from a main-reservoir-pipe connection to a train-pipe connection.

If operated correctly the air-brake system is

fail-safe. However, in the past there have been accidents resulting from careless operation, often leading to runaways. Two possible causes are highlighted below.

The first scenario is if one of the end cocks on the train pipe is left closed when vehicles are coupled together to make a train formation. As a result the air pressure does not get through to the back of the train, and the auxiliary reservoirs are not charged with air, as shown in **Figure 10.12**.

The portion of the train between the isolated air cock and the end without a locomotive has no brake pressure. The more vehicles that have no brake pressure, the less likely the train will stop. As a result, station over-runs and collisions could occur.

Fortunately the above scenario can be avoided by performing a continuity test. The driver's control valve is set to its release position to charge the train pipe with air, and another member of the train staff opens the end cock on the last vehicle of the train. If air

comes out of the end cock it is verified that there are no blockages and the entire train is being supplied with air. The continuity test should be carried out whenever a new train formation is made up.

The second scenario is if air pressure becomes trapped in the air system of vehicles that are being uncoupled from a train formation. This occurs if the driver has not released all the pressure from the train pipe at the time when the vehicles are uncoupled. When the end cocks are shut so that the pipes can be disconnected, any air pressure that is in the train pipe will become trapped, as shown in **Figure 10.13**.

The uncoupled vehicles are thus left with their brakes either fully or partially released. If they are left on a gradient any minor disturbance could then cause them to roll away. To avoid this the driver should ensure that all the air pressure is emptied from the train pipe when vehicles are to be uncoupled. In addition, the member of staff uncoupling

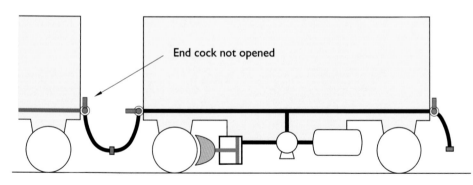

End cock not opened

Auxiliary reservoir empty

Figure 10.12
Dangerous scenario – vehicles with *no* brake pressure

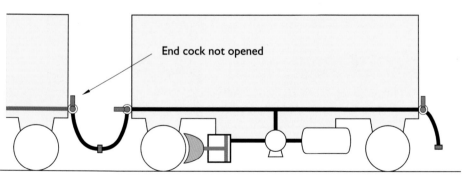

End cock not opened

Auxiliary reservoir empty

Figure 10.13
Dangerous scenario – vehicles with trapped air

the vehicles can check that there is no trapped air. Once the end hoses are disconnected, the end cock on the uncoupled vehicles should be reopened to let out any trapped air pressure.

Vacuum brakes

Vacuum brakes are an alternative to the air brakes described previously. The vacuum brake uses air from the atmosphere, to push against a piston in a cylinder, to provide the force to push the brake block against the wheel, as shown in **Figure 10.14**. The air at atmospheric pressure is only effective when a vacuum is present on the other side of the piston.

As with air brakes, every brake block is fitted to a brake hanger link, which prevents it from trying to move round with the wheel.

For the vacuum-brake system to function, air has to be sucked out of the cylinder and then a vacuum retained on one side of the piston. This is achieved by a non-return valve fitted to the head of the piston, as shown in **Figure 10.15**. When air is sucked from the bottom of the cylinder, the non-return valve is held open and air is also sucked from the top of the piston, as shown in the left-hand diagram. With a vacuum on both sides, the piston will fall under the influence of gravity to the bottom of the cylinder. When air at atmospheric pressure is admitted back into the bottom of the cylinder, the non-return valve is forced shut, trapping a vacuum on the upper side of the piston, as shown in the right-hand diagram. With a vacuum on top the piston will be forced upwards by the atmospheric air pressure underneath.

The area above the piston is commonly referred to as the vacuum chamber.

As explained in relation to air brakes, all passenger trains must have a fail-safe braking system whereby all the brakes are applied automatically if the train becomes separated into two parts (*i.e.* continuous brakes). The vacuum-brake system was devised to provide the required fail-safe measure by fitting every vehicle of the train with vacuum-brake cylinders and connecting them together by a pipe running along the whole length of the train. This is known as the train-brake pipe. Between each vehicle are flexible end hoses, to allow vehicle brakes to be joined

Figure 10.14
Vacuum brake – brakes *applied*

Figure 10.15
Vacuum brake cylinder

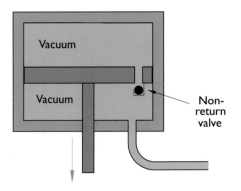

Brake RELEASED

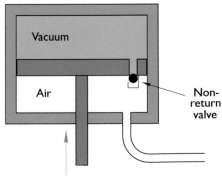

Brake APPLIED

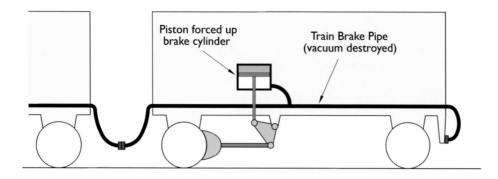

Figure 10.16
Vehicle with brakes
released

Figure 10.17
Vehicle with brakes
applied

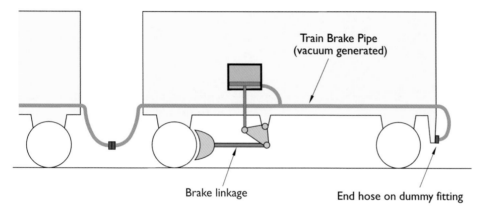

and separated. The air is sucked from the train-brake pipe by the locomotive, as shown in **Figure 10.16**. The end hoses between the vehicles must all be connected so that air is sucked from the entire train, whilst the end vehicles in the train are made to retain the vacuum by placing the end hoses on a dummy fitting. In this condition there is a vacuum present on both sides of the piston inside the brake cylinder. The piston falls to the bottom of the cylinder under the influence of gravity, and thus moves the brake blocks away from the wheels via the brake linkage.

When air is allowed into the train-brake pipe, as shown in **Figure 10.17**, a vacuum is retained above the pistons in all of the brake cylinders. The pressure of the air from the atmosphere underneath the piston forces it up the cylinder, and the brakes are applied via the brake linkage.

• The driver reduces the train pipe vacuum to apply the brakes.

• The driver increases the train pipe vacuum to release the brakes.

If a coupling breaks, the end hoses are pulled apart and air enters the train pipe from the surrounding atmosphere. Hence, the train brakes are all applied in the event of the train becoming separated. However, once stationary the stored vacuum will very gradually leak away, so the train must be secured by a handbrake or chocks (called 'scotches' in railway terminology) if it is to be left for more than a few minutes.

The amount of air allowed into the train-brake pipe from the atmosphere effectively controls the severity of the braking. The more atmospheric air that is allowed into the train-brake pipe, the greater the air pressure forcing each brake piston to rise, and the greater the brake force exerted by the brake blocks against the wheels. A vacuum-brake cylinder as fitted underneath a passenger carriage is seen in **Figure 10.18**.

Figure 10.18
This typical vacuum-brake cylinder is underneath a carriage. The painted white star identifies its location to the train crew, and, should it be necessary to release or ease the vacuum from the upper side of the piston, this can be carried out locally to each cylinder.

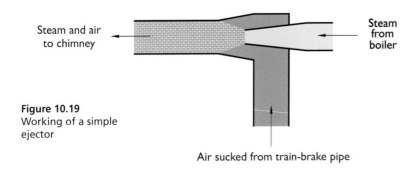

Steam and air to chimney

Steam from boiler

Air sucked from train-brake pipe

Figure 10.19
Working of a simple ejector

The vacuum to operate the brakes has to be created by the locomotive. This is typically achieved by a device known as the ejector. Steam at high pressure from the boiler is accelerated to high speed through a cone, as shown in **Figure 10.19**. The exit from this cone is surrounded by a passage connected to the train-brake pipe. The steam leaving the cone is directed into an exhaust pipe which leads to the locomotive's chimney. As the steam leaves the cone at high speed it draws air from the surrounding chamber along with it. Thus air is sucked from the train-brake pipe.

Note that the principle of the ejector (using steam to draw air from the train-brake pipe) is exactly the same as that of the blastpipe (using exhaust steam to draw the flames from the fire to the smokebox). An ejector is often seen just in front of the cab alongside the boiler, as in **Figure 10.20**.

From the ejector the connection to the train-brake pipe is via a non-return valve. This prevents air from entering the train-brake pipe through the ejector when the ejector is not in operation (for example if two locomotives are double-heading).

Figure 10.20
This vacuum-brake ejector is situated just ahead of the cab on a GWR locomotive. Steam is supplied through the copper pipes from the control valves in the cab, and air is sucked from the train brake pipe via the large green pipe. The exhaust of steam and air heads towards the chimney, which is out of sight to the right.

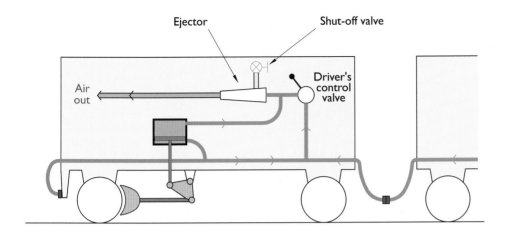

Figure 10.21
Locomotive with brakes *released*

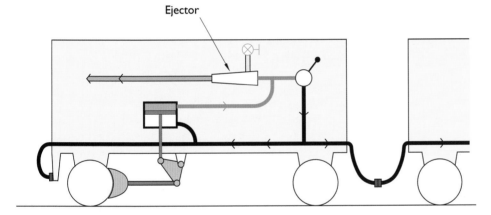

Figure 10.22
Locomotive with brakes *applied*

From the non-return valve the connection to the train-brake pipe passes through the driver's control valve, as shown in **Figure 10.21**. Air is drawn out of the train-brake pipe in the directions indicated by the arrowheads on the diagram, and the brakes are released.

When a brake application is required the driver's control valve is operated. This control valve closes the connection between the ejector and the train-brake pipe, and allows air at atmospheric pressure into the train-brake pipe, as shown in **Figure 10.22**. Air rushes into the train-brake pipe in the directions indicated by the arrowheads on the diagram, and the brakes are applied.

Note that on locomotives fitted with vacuum-brake cylinders there is usually an additional connection from the ejector (and its associated non-return valve) directly to the vacuum chamber of the brake cylinder. This ensures that when the train is braking, at least the locomotive's vacuum chamber always has the maximum possible vacuum.

On some locomotives the ejector, ejector steam valve and brake controller are combined in a single fitting in the cab. On other locomotives these components are independent fittings that are connected by pipes.

The cab of the locomotive is fitted with vacuum gauges connected to both the train-brake pipe and the locomotive's vacuum chamber, as seen in **Figure 10.23**. From this the driver will know the severity of any brake application.

Vacuum-brake systems are generally considered to be simpler than air-brake systems, and are particularly reliable because the ejector component has no complex moving parts, unlike its counterpart the air pump. However, the vacuum-brake system is

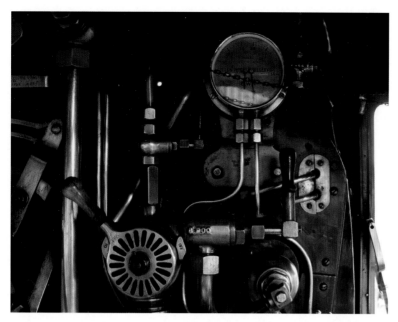

Figure 10.23
The vacuum-brake
controls of a large
GWR locomotive. The
large wooden handle
attached to the
serrated disc is moved
to allow air into the
train-brake pipe.
The smaller handle to
the right is opened to
allow steam from the
boiler to the ejector in
order to suck air from
the train brake pipe.
The gauge above the
handles has two
needles, which indicate
the train pipe vacuum
and the locomotive's
chamber vacuum.

Figure 10.24
The small cylinder
above the wheels is the
vacuum pump, as used
on GWR locomotives.
The pump's piston rod
is directly connected to
the crosshead of the
main steam cylinder.

more susceptible to small leaks in the system
and therefore it is not as easy to retain a
vacuum as to retain a high air pressure. As a
result the ejector is running all the time to
retain the vacuum in the train pipe, and thus
uses more steam than an air pump and hence
more fuel is burned by the locomotive.

To overcome some of the shortcomings of
the vacuum-brake system some locomotives
are fitted with vacuum pumps. These are
simple mechanical pumps, which are driven by
a connection to the external moving parts of
the steam locomotive, as seen in **Figure 10.24**.

The vacuum pump generates a vacuum
whenever the locomotive is moving. It is
connected to the brake system as shown in
Figure 10.25. The ejector is used to suck air from
the train pipe whilst the locomotive is stationary,
and, once it is underway, the vacuum pump
sucks air from the train-brake pipe, making up
for any leakages in the system. The ejector can
then be turned off, to conserve steam.

When it is required to make a brake
application, air is allowed into the train-brake
pipe through the driver's control valve.
However, if the vacuum pump is fitted directly
onto the train-brake pipe there will be the
tendency for it to try and fight the brake
application by continuing to suck air from the
train-brake pipe whilst the driver's brake valve
is admitting air. For this reason the vacuum-
brake pump is often connected indirectly to the
train-brake pipe via a retaining valve. When

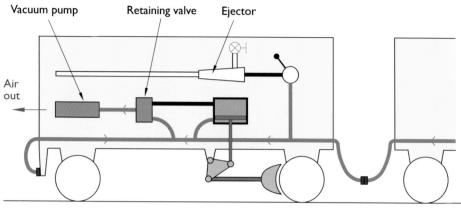

Figure 10.25
Locomotive with
vacuum pump and
brakes *released*

Figure 10.26
Locomotive with
vacuum pump
andbrakes *applied*

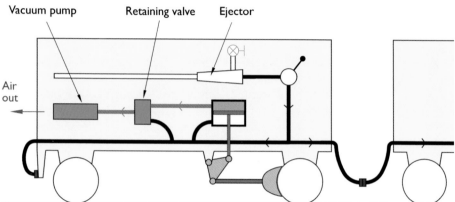

there is a reduction in vacuum in the train-brake pipe (*i.e.* during a brake application) the retaining valve automatically redirects the suck from the vacuum pump to the vacuum chamber of the locomotive instead of the train-brake pipe, as shown in **Figure 10.26**. When it is required to re-release the brakes, the driver will have to turn on the ejector to suck air out of the train-brake pipe. When the vacuum has been fully re-created the retaining valve automatically redirects the suck from the vacuum pump to the train-brake pipe, and then the ejector can be turned off.

Vacuum pumps were fitted to many of the former Great Western Railway (GWR) locomotives, and the brakes therefore require a little more skill to operate, because the driver has to alternately operate both the ejector steam valve and the driver's control valve.

The vacuum-brake system is less prone to accidental incorrect set-up than the air-brake system previously described. There are no isolating cocks on the ends of the vehicles, so it is not possible to trap a vacuum in the train-brake pipe of vehicles being uncoupled from the locomotive. The end vacuum pipe simply sucks itself onto a dummy fitting during operation, and the vacuum is destroyed immediately when any of the joined hoses are pulled apart. However, it is still possible to make a train formation and leave some of the vehicles without a brake, by not connecting all the end hoses. As a result these vehicles are unable to store any vacuum in their vacuum chambers, as shown in **Figure 10.27**. The portion of the train between the unconnected brake-pipe hoses and the end without a locomotive has no brake. The more vehicles that have no brake, the less likely the train will stop; station over-runs and collisions could result.

Fortunately this scenario can be avoided by performing a continuity test. The driver's control valve is set to its release position to create a vacuum in the train-brake pipe, and

Figure 10.27
Dangerous scenario –
vehicles with *no* brake

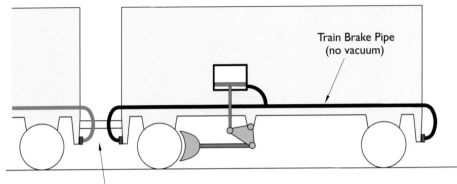

Train Brake Pipe
(no vacuum)

Vehicles coupled but brake hoses not connected

another member of the train staff should verify that a vacuum is present at the opposite end of the train. If there is no vacuum gauge present (*i.e.* as fitted in a guard's van or compartment) then the hose at the end of the train can be momentarily left off its dummy fitting. If air is being sucked in through this end hose then it is verified that there are no serious blockages and hence vacuum is being generated over the entire length of the train. The continuity test should be carried out whenever a new train formation is made up.

Independent locomotive brakes

The previous sections have described systems of continuous train brakes, powered by compressed air or by vacuum.

Most locomotives are fitted with additional brakes. For example almost all steam locomotives have a handbrake, which is primarily used to secure the locomotive when on shed and the train brake system is not turned on (*i.e.* there is no air pressure or vacuum in the system). This type of brake is completely independent from the train-brake system and can also be used to hold a train stationary during short station stops. The train brake can then be released well in advance of the departure. This is particularly useful with the vacuum-brake system, whereby it may take a minute or so to release fully the brakes of a long train.

The direct air brake is another system that is independent from the train brake. On locomotives fitted with the air-brake system the direct air valve simply admits air straight from the main air reservoir to the locomotive's brake cylinders, as shown in **Figure 10.28**. This is useful as a parking brake during station stops and also when shunting the locomotive, as it gives a quicker response than using the train brake. A double check valve ensures that the

Figure 10.28
Direct air brake *applied*

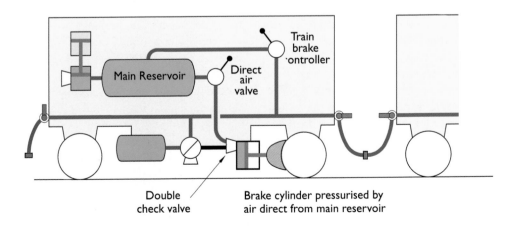

Train
brake
controller

Direct
air
valve

Main Reservoir

Double
check valve

Brake cylinder pressurised by
air direct from main reservoir

brake cylinder can be pressurised with air from either the direct air brake or the train-brake system. In this way the locomotive's brakes will still be applied in unison with the train brake.

The direct air brake is purely a supplementary means of applying the locomotive's brakes only. There is a completely separate control handle placed in the cab, as seen in **Figure 10.29**.

A very similar type of independent brake used on steam locomotives is the steam brake. This admits steam direct from the boiler to the locomotive's brake cylinders, as shown in **Figure 10.30**. Unlike the direct air brake, the steam-brake system has dedicated steam-brake cylinders which are not supplied with air pressure or vacuum from the train brake system.

Figure 10.29
In the cab of 'A1' Pacific locomotive Tornado can be seen the train air-brake controller (nearest camera) and the direct air-brake valve (just above).

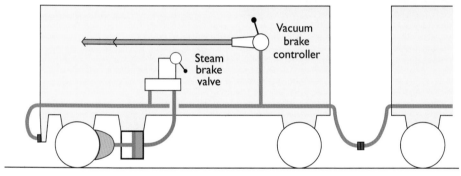

Brake cylinder pressurised by steam direct from the boiler

Figure 10.30
Steam brake *applied*

Figure 10.31
Great Central Railway fitter James Hazell tests the operation of the steam-brake valve on BR Standard locomotive No 78019, using the external handle. The vacuum brake controller is just below.

The steam brake can however work in complete unison with either the air brake or vacuum-brake systems (the latter is shown in the diagram). The steam-brake valve is connected to the train-brake pipe and will automatically admit steam to the brake cylinders when it senses that there is a drop in vacuum in the train-brake pipe. Similarly, the steam-brake valve will automatically release pressure from the brake cylinders when it senses that a vacuum is generated in the train-brake pipe.

The steam-brake valve is also fitted with a control handle, seen in **Figure 10.31**, which will override the train brake and allow the locomotive's brakes to be applied regardless of the vacuum in the train-brake pipe. This makes it possible to use the steam brake for shunting the locomotive and as a parking brake during short station stops.

Chapter 11

Locomotive Controls

Control valves

For a steam locomotive to operate successfully there has to be a means of controlling the steam generated by the boiler, the water flowing from the tanks, and the air pressure used for the brakes. This is achieved using control valves, and there are many different types. Essentially all these valves are used to either permit the flow of gas or liquid through pipes or to prevent it, whichever is required by the crew at that point in time. Some of the more typical types of control valve are detailed below.

Sliding-face valve

This consists of a flat plate with a hole in it. The plate slides over a surface incorporating an outlet pipe, as shown in **Figure 11.1**. When closed, the pressure of steam from the boiler keeps the plate pressed hard against the flat surface, and thus prevents leaks.

The sliding-face type of valve is typically used for the regulator on steam locomotives, which allows large amounts of steam to leave the boiler and pass to the cylinders. The sliding-face valve is ideal for the regulator because it can be made with large passages (thus providing the minimum resistance to the steam flow) and because it can be closed very quickly (for example in an emergency-stop situation).

Disc valve

This uses the same principle as the sliding-face valve. A flat disc with a hole in it rotates over a surface incorporating an outlet pipe, as shown in **Figure 11.2**. When the disc is closed the pressure of steam from the boiler keeps it pressed hard against the flat surface and thus prevents leaks.

As well as being quick in action the disc valve can incorporate multiple holes and/or multiple outlets. By this means steam can be directed into different passages, which are uncovered as the handle is rotated. This makes it ideal for use in applications such as steam sanding valves, for example, where one handle can be used to select sanding for both forward and backward directions.

Disc valves are also commonly used as the basis for brake controllers. In this application it is air pressure that is used to keep the disc pressed hard against the flat surface.

Figure 11.1
Sliding-face valve

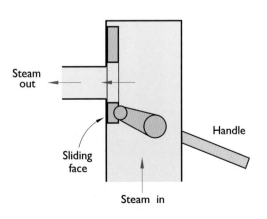

Valve OPEN

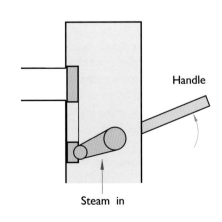

Valve CLOSED

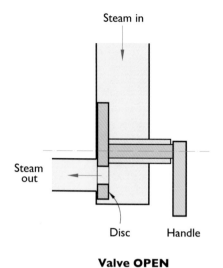

Steam in

Steam
out

Disc   Handle

Valve OPEN

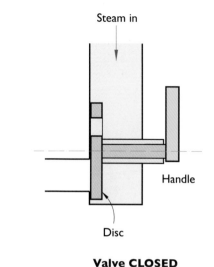

Steam in

Handle

Disc

Valve CLOSED

Figure 11.2
Disc valve

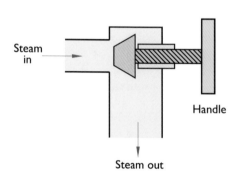

Steam
in

Handle

Steam out

Valve OPEN

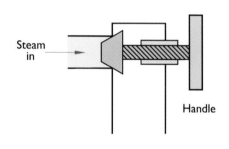

Steam
in

Handle

Valve CLOSED

Figure 11.3
Screw-down valve

Figure 11.4
These two handles control the blower and the steam sander. The blower valve is on the left and is of the screw-down type, which gives fine adjustment of its steam supply and hence the draught on the fire, but it requires several turns to open fully. The sander valve is of the sliding-face type, because it has to be quick-acting and allow for selection of forward and reverse steam sanders. It requires only a quarter-turn in either direction to open, but there is no regulation over the steam supply; it is all or nothing.

Screw-down valve

This incorporates a taper plug fitting, which can be screwed firmly onto an inlet passage to control steam flow, as shown in **Figure 11.3**. When fully screwed down the plug forms a tight fit in the inlet pipe, preventing any leaks.

The screw-down valve is probably the most common type of valve fitted on steam locomotives, mainly because of its reliable steam-tightness when closed. This type of valve also provides very fine control over the steam flow, as it can severely restrict the steam flow when it is only partially opened. This makes it ideal for use as a blower control valve, for example, by providing the operator with the ability to select just how much steam is allowed to the blower nozzles, and

thence a precise control over the draught on the fire.

An installation consisting of a screw-down valve and a sliding-surface-type valve is seen in **Figure 11.4**.

Ball valve

This has an internal ball with a steam passage bored through it, as shown in **Figure 11.5**. When opened, the passage is in line with the

Figure 11.5
Ball valve

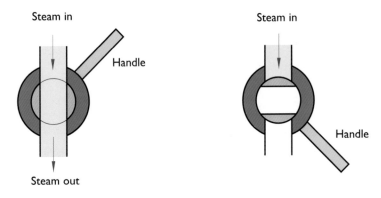

Steam in

Handle

Steam out

Valve OPEN

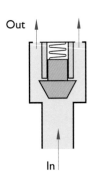

Out

Spring

In

Valve OPEN

Steam in

Handle

Valve CLOSED

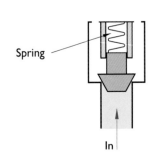

In

Valve CLOSED

Figure 11.5
Ball valve

Figure 11.6
Safety valve

Figure 11.7
These two fittings are safety valves. The central spring applies a closing force on the valves via the beam across the top

steam pipe, and steam flows very freely through it. When closed, the passage is at right angles to the steam pipe, and the sides of the ball fitting effectively block the steam flow.

The ball valve is a modern development, and as such it is not as common to find on steam locomotives as the other types of valve described. However, its quick and simple action has made it popular to retrofit for many of the auxiliary fittings, such as injector steam and water valves.

Safety valve / relief valve

To prevent the boiler (or any pressure vessel) from exceeding its maximum safe working pressure, it is crucial to fit safety valves (also frequently known as relief valves). They consist of a taper plug or a flat face or sometimes a small ball, which is pressed hard onto a steam inlet pipe by a mechanical spring, as shown in **Figure 11.6**. They are automatic in action, the spring being adjusted so that it applies the same force to the top of the plug as the maximum safe working pressure applied underneath the plug. Thus, when the pressure is less than the maximum safe working pressure, the spring force holds the valve shut. When the pressure reaches the maximum for safe working the spring is unable to hold the valve shut, and hence the pressure is released.

At least two safety valves are fitted to every steam locomotive boiler, as seen in **Figure 11.7**.

Although the principle is always the same, there are variations in how safety valves may function. When opened fully they waste a large amount of steam and hence the fuel used to generate that steam is also wasted. Therefore, some safety valves are designed to open very gradually as the maximum steam pressure is approached, thus alerting the crew and giving them chance to slightly reduce the boiler pressure and hence prevent

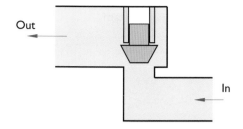

Out

In

Valve OPEN

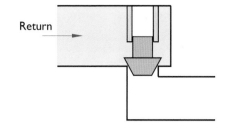

Return

Valve CLOSED

Figure 11.8
Non-return valve

the waste of a large volume of steam. When safety valves open very gradually like this they are said to be 'feathering'. An alternative type of safety valve is the 'pop' valve, which does not release any pressure until the maximum safe working pressure is about to be exceeded. They then release steam very quickly until the pressure has been reduced by a fixed amount. The 'pop'-type safety valve allows the crew to work the boiler closer to its maximum safe working pressure without wasting steam.

Safety valves are also fitted to air and vacuum-brake systems. In the case of air brakes, the safety valve prevents excessive air pressure from bursting pipes, reservoirs and fittings. In the case of vacuum brakes, the safety valve prevents excessive vacuum from collapsing these parts in on themselves.

Non-return valve

There are many circumstances where a flow of steam, water or air is desired in one direction only, and to make this possible a non-return valve is fitted. This consists of a taper plug or a flat face or sometimes a small ball, which is pressed hard onto an inlet pipe by any pressure that is present on its outlet side, as shown in **Figure 11.8**. Non-return valves are automatic in action. When the pressure on the inlet side of the valve exceeds that on the outlet side, the valve is opened and gas or liquid flows through it. When there is no pressure on the inlet side, the valve is pressed shut by the pressure on the outlet side, preventing any flow.

Non-return valves are used in conjunction with the injectors, where they prevent steam in the boiler from escaping back down the water

delivery pipe when the injector is turned off. In this application they are called 'clack valves', and an example is seen in **Figure 11.9**.

Similarly, non-return valves are used in conjunction with air-brake pumps and vacuum-brake ejectors. On locomotives with air brakes, non-return valves are used to prevent air pressure escaping from the main air reservoir when the pump is turned off. On locomotives with vacuum brakes, non-return valves are used to prevent air from re-entering the vacuum chambers once it has been sucked out.

Cab layouts

There are many different cab layouts on steam locomotives, but the basic controls are always the same. On any given locomotive the detailed fittings such as the whistle handle and drain cocks lever could be in any suitable position. The position of such controls may

Figure 11.9
This fitting houses a pair of clack valves. Pressurised feed water enters from the adjacent copper pipes and is delivered into the boiler below.

Figure 11.10
The driver's side of the cab on ex-Great Central Railway locomotive No 63601, with the regulator handle, screw-reverser and vacuum-brake controller all easily identifiable.

also have been modified at some time or other to suit a railway's operating requirements. However, the main controls usually follow a similar basic pattern and are easily identified. **Figure 11.10** shows the driver's side of a locomotive cab.

A series of cab layouts is now illustrated to show what is typically found on the footplate of a steam locomotive.

The first cab layout, **Figure 11.11**, illustrates a typical industrial locomotive. The fireman usually stands on the left and the driver on the right. This is the optimum arrangement for a right-handed fireman to shovel coal into the firebox.

In industrial locomotives it is common to find the main controls arranged so that the locomotive can be driven from either side when shunting. In such cases the regulator handle is extended to both sides of the cab and there may be a duplicate brake controller. However, the reversing lever is rarely duplicated, so the fireman may be required to assist the driver by operating this control.

The second cab layout, **Figure 11.12**, illustrates a locomotive of the Great Western Railway (GWR). The GWR was unique among the pre-nationalisation railway companies in having a standard cab layout on its locomotives. Whether boarding an express passenger locomotive, a freight locomotive or a shunting locomotive, the crew always found the same basic layout of the main controls.

As with the previous cab layout, the fireman is on the left and the driver is on the right. An unusual feature is the presence of only one gauge glass, which is backed up by try-cocks as part of the same fitting. The injector water valves and the handbrake are not shown, as they would be situated at the

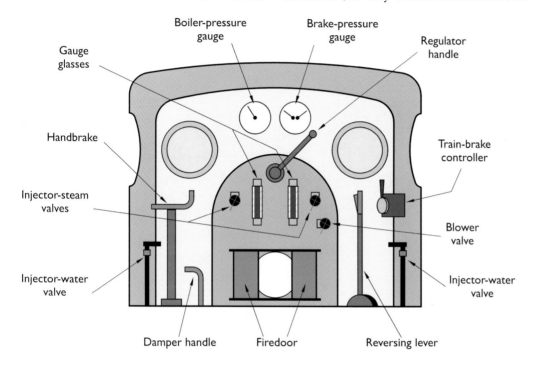

Figure 11.11
Typical cab of industrial shunting locomotive

Boiler-pressure gauge

Brake-pressure gauge

Regulator handle

Gauge glasses

Handbrake

Train-brake controller

Injector-steam valves

Injector-water valve

Blower valve

Injector-water valve

Damper handle

Firedoor

Reversing lever

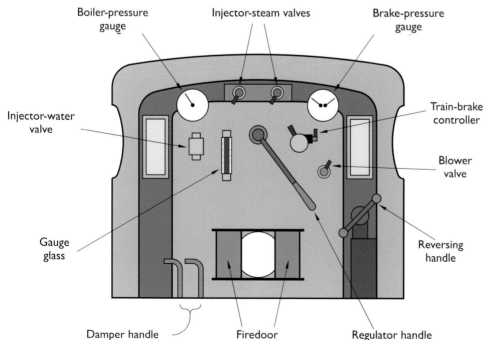

Figure 11.12
Standard cab of Great Western Railway locomotive

Boiler-pressure gauge

Injector-steam valves

Brake-pressure gauge

Injector-water valve

Train-brake controller

Blower valve

Gauge glass

Reversing handle

Damper handle

Firedoor

Regulator handle

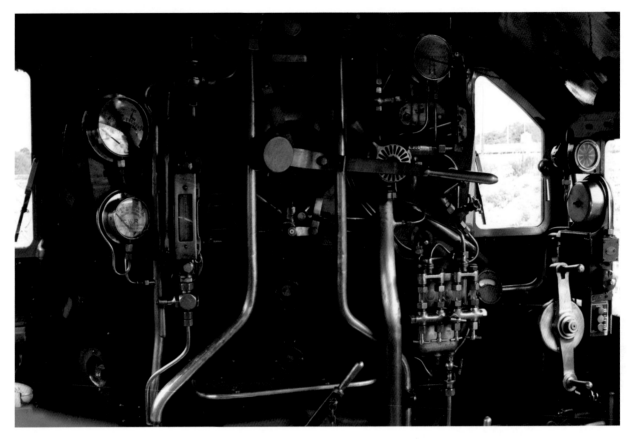

Figure 11.13
The cab of ex-GWR locomotive Rood Ashton Hall appears complicated owing to the large number of steam pipes. However, the layout of controls is basically the same as in Figure 11.12. The placing of so many steam pipes within the cab gives the exterior of the locomotive a clean, uncluttered appearance.

Figure 11.14
Cab of British Standard locomotive

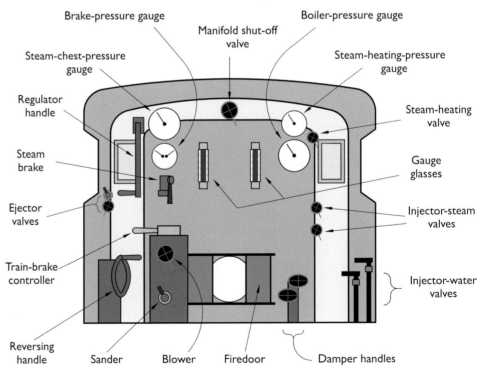

Brake-pressure gauge

Manifold shut-off valve

Boiler-pressure gauge

Steam-chest-pressure gauge

Steam-heating-pressure gauge

Regulator handle

Steam-heating valve

Steam brake

Gauge glasses

Ejector valves

Injector-steam valves

Train-brake controller

Injector-water valves

Reversing handle

Sander

Blower

Firedoor

Damper handles

rear of the cab or on the tender. Compare Figure 11.12 with **Figure 11.13**, showing an actual GWR locomotive cab.

The final cab layout, **Figure 11.14**, illustrates the arrangement used by British Railways for its standard steam locomotives, built following nationalisation. On these locomotives the driver is seated on the left, to allow optimum viewing of signals when running chimney first, whilst the fireman is on the right. This cab layout represents considerable evolution of the steam locomotive, with all the controls conveniently located for each crew member, as seen in **Figure 11.15**. Both injectors are controlled from the fireman's side of the cab, whilst the blower control is easily accessed by either the driver or the fireman.

Figure 11.15
The fireman's side of the cab on BR Standard locomotive No 78019, with the various steam valves all conveniently positioned for the fireman.

TENDER SPRAY

Chapter 12

The Role of the Driver and Fireman

Progression

The typical path to becoming a fireman or driver of steam locomotives is as follows:

1. Induction into the health and safety principles of working on the railway.

2. Training in general maintenance work on shed, to gain an understanding of the arrangement and components of the steam locomotive.

3. Development of theoretical knowledge of the steam locomotive.

4. Cleaner – responsible for helping loco crews to prepare their locomotive at the start of the day and to make it presentable for passenger service.

5. Learning the procedures for safe operation of the trains from the railway's custom Rule Book.

6. Trainee fireman – using every opportunity to learn the practical skills from experienced crews and build up good route knowledge. The trainee must gain the skills required in the management of the boiler and the safe operation of the trains.

7. Fireman – responsible for management of the locomotive boiler from preparation through to disposal, whenever they are rostered on the footplate. May also be called upon to train others following in their footsteps.

8. Trainee driver – typically starting with exposure to the controls on light-engine runs and empty-coaching-stock workings. Must be accompanied by further understanding of the working of the steam locomotive, route knowledge and procedures in the Rule Book.

9. Driver – responsible for the safe operation of the locomotive and supervision of the fireman, whenever they are rostered on the footplate. May also be called upon to train others following in their footsteps.

Teamwork

The driver, fireman and their trainees are a team. Although this may seem obvious, it is only by mutual respect and co-operation of this team that the steam locomotive can successfully do its work.

The *driver* is the leader of the team, with the most experience and with the overall responsibility for the locomotive and its crew. A good driver will convey confidence to the fireman and any trainees, giving praise where due, advice when required based on their experience, and will also look out for the safety of the footplate crew.

The *fireman* is the key to successful operation of the locomotive, and is continually learning how to get the best performance out of the locomotive with the variation in the fuel supplied. A good fireman will convey confidence to any trainees, giving praise where due and advice based on experience when required.

The *trainees* are the future of steam-locomotive operation. A good trainee will absorb the teachings of the passed-out drivers and firemen, and should not be afraid to have an open mind to suggestions made by a variety of more experienced crew members. The trainees will make mistakes on their route to gaining experience, and in a good team this learning of new skills will be very fulfilling.

Whether a driver supervising a fireman in normal duties, or a fireman supervising a trainee, the key skills are to determine the capabilities of the less experienced crew members through observation, then to allow them to learn by a combination of hands-on experience, advice on how to overcome minor mistakes, and by only stepping in where there is a risk to the successful and safe operation of the locomotive.

Inevitably drivers and firemen do not always see eye to eye, but what they always have in common is a special interest in the steam locomotive and a desire to operate it in the best possible way.

It is the etiquette of the locomotive crew that makes the difference between a good or bad day on a steam locomotive, and not the steaming performance of the locomotive itself.

Chapter 13

Preparation of Locomotives

Starting the preparation

Locomotive crews usually arrive several hours before the first train departure. The procedure for preparing the locomotive and the division of duties between the driver, fireman and any cleaners will vary with the practice on each independent railway. However, it is the driver who is ultimately responsible for ensuring that the locomotive is fully prepared for its intended duty. The following sections outline the typical collective tasks carried out by the crew.

1. Check that the locomotive is in a suitable position for the preparation and lighting up to take place. Check that the handbrake is firmly applied.

2. Ensure that the water level in the boiler is present in the visible part of the gauge glasses. Drain the gauge glasses and check that the water level rises back into the glass.

3. Remove the chimney lid (where fitted).

4. Open the firehole door and inspect the firebox for leaks, including the condition of the superheater elements and the fusible plugs. Check that the brick arch is intact.

5. Open the smokebox door and check the tubes and tubeplate for leaks. Brush out the tubes and use a shovel to clear out excessive char and soot from the bottom of the smokebox. Check that the sealing ring around the smokebox door is intact. Close the smokebox door tightly to prevent loss of vacuum during operation.

6. Verify that there is a sufficient level of water in the tanks, fuel in the bunker and plenty of sand in the sandboxes. If necessary these should be topped up at the first opportunity.

Lighting a coal fire

1. In addition to the smokebox checks above, clean the spark-arrestor mesh and baffle plates (where fitted). These may need to be temporarily removed whilst accessing the tubes.

2. Clean out the remains of the previous fire by use of the fire irons and/or rocking grate.

3. If possible empty the ashpan. If not, check that the ash is not touching the firebars, as too much debris in the ashpan will hinder steaming and could lead to the firebars overheating.

4. On locomotives with large fireboxes, shovel a thin layer of coal around the grate. On locomotives with very small fireboxes this is not necessary.

5. Start the fire with waste wood and a lit rag placed into the middle of the firebox. For large fireboxes it may be necessary to start several small fires in this way.

6. Gradually build up the fire with coal, keeping smoke to a minimum and using compressed air assistance for the draught if necessary. The boiler pressure will eventually rise. When there is sufficient boiler pressure, the steam blower can be brought into use for creating the required draught.

Lighting an oil-burner

The following procedure describes the specific tasks required to light an oil-burner. It may be helpful to refer back to the diagrams in Chapter 4.

1. Check the oil level, and check the visible oil pipes and valves for leaks.

2. Check that the burner is free from carbon deposits. If necessary, gently knock off any such deposits using a wooden pole or a stiff brush.

3. Ensure that the main oil shut-off valve is closed, then take out and clean the oil filter. This is located downstream of the shut-off valve. When clean, place the filter back in position.

4. Check that the steam manifold valve is closed and then connect the compressed air supply.

5. Close the drain valve.

6. Open the main oil shut-off valve.

7. Gently open the blower valve to clear out any condensate from the boiler. Leave the blower valve partially open.

8. Push a lit rag into the firebox through the small chute in the firedoor.

9. Whilst observing the atomiser-pressure gauge turn the atomiser valve up until there is a moderate pressure, so that the atomising air is just audible and ensuring that the rag remains lit.

10. Turn on the oil-control valve, and the burner should light after a few seconds.
    If the fire does not ignite, shut the oil valve and seek advice. Remember that a firebox full of atomised oil is highly explosive.

11. When the burner is lit, adjust the blower, atomiser and oil-control valves to give the minimum smoke emission.

The exact technique for lighting an oil-burner, including the knowledge of the required valve openings, is learned through appropriate training and experience that is provided by railways that have adopted oil firing.

When lighting a cold locomotive the fireman should not heat up the boiler too quickly, as this can cause unnecessary stresses to its structure. Therefore the oil-burner is either set with a very low flame, or a dedicated procedure is followed whereby the burner is turned out for set periods of time.

Cleaning, inspection and oiling round

1. Clean the fittings with brass cleaner, starting with those that will get hot as the locomotive generates steam, for example the gauge-glass fittings. Note that brass cleaner is also very effective for cleaning glazed areas, including the cab windows, pressure-gauge faces and gauge glasses.

2. Wipe over the paintwork both externally and inside the cab. If it is particularly filthy the addition of a suitable cleaning fluid will help remove any grime, as seen in Figure 13.1. However, note that the application of a cleaning fluid can attract dirt unless it is thoroughly polished off.

3. Inspect the frames and motion work for loose pins or other faults. Clean the motion work using a suitable rag. A stiff brush dipped in a bucket of diesel will help to remove any grime.

4. Wipe all the lubrication points and then carry out the greasing and oiling required for that particular locomotive. Figure 13.2 shows the driver topping up the mechanical lubricators prior to departure. Details of the individual requirements of each locomotive are usually provided in appropriate log books.

Figure 13.1
Driver John Bell and fireman Graham Pattison clean the exterior of Welsh Highland Railway locomotive No K1 prior to the day's duties. The fine results of this preparation can be seen in the photograph in Chapter 5.

5. Top up and clean the oil cans and also ensure that there is a sufficient supply of clean rags on the footplate for use during the day.

Preparing to go 'off shed'

1. Clear the footplate of any unnecessary tools and equipment, so as to provide a clear and safe working space.

2. When the full boiler pressure is obtained, blow through the gauge glasses to ensure that there are no blockages. Instructions regarding the use of gauge glasses are given in the Water Management chapter.

3. Test the operation of all the valves (including both injectors) to ensure that everything is fully functional.

4. It is good practice to take the boiler right up to full pressure and let it blow off. This will verify that the safety valves are functioning correctly.

5. Attend to any water treatment requirements, such as the addition of chemicals into the water tanks and operation of the blow-down valve. The requirements of boiler water treatment vary depending on the exact method employed.

6. Turn on the locomotive brake system (air, vacuum or steam) and test its correct function before releasing the handbrake.

7. Check for any special instructions, including speed restrictions and the location of any scheduled track gangs working on the line

Figure 13.2
Before heading a passenger train up the line, the fireman checks that ash is clear of the firebars while the driver tops up the lubricators.

On the Line

Chapter 14

Description of coal firing

The coal fireman is expected to generate the required amount of steam to haul the train, whilst creating the minimum amount of smoke at the chimney.

On stepping onto a coal-fired locomotive the fireman will check whether the water level and fire are sufficient for the work about to be carried out. If steep gradients are ahead, it will be necessary to build up the fire and raise the water level. This is typically carried out during a station stop or during gentle coasting. The blower is turned up to provide more draught through the firebox, and more coal is added to the fire. This generates more steam and raises the boiler pressure. The fireman can then turn on one of the injectors to force water into the boiler, thereby steadily increasing the water level. When the injector is running, the boiler pressure tends to fall due to steam being used to power the injector, and to the influx of cold water. If the fire is burning well it is possible to generate enough excess steam to balance the running of the injector, and the boiler pressure holds steady whilst water is forced into the boiler. In these circumstances the fire must be steadily replenished with coal.

With the fire roaring the locomotive is steadily warmed up ready to work hard. The fireman has to use judgement and increasing experience (of locomotive and route) to choose the right time to turn on the blower and add coal to the fire. If the fire is built up too early, or the train is delayed from leaving a station, the fireman must be cautious not to force too much water into the boiler as this can result in priming. In such cases it may be necessary to ease back with the blower and/or allow the safety valves to lift and thus release the pressure. Unfortunately it is usually not possible to turn off the blower, because the fresh coal on the fire would simply create thick smoke at the chimney, as well as presenting a blowback risk.

When the driver opens the regulator the resulting exhaust steam from the cylinders generates more draught on the fire, which thus becomes hotter and generates more steam. In this way, coal-fired locomotives are semi-automatic in their function: the harder the work demanded, the hotter the fire becomes. However, there is a noticeable delay in these events' taking place, hence the prior use of the blower if the locomotive is about to be worked hard. Note that the fireman is still in total control of the amount of coal that is added to the fire.

When the locomotive is working steadily the fireman checks that the fire is generating a slight excess of steam, shown by a steady rise on the boiler-pressure gauge. The excess steam can then be used to intermittently run the injectors and feed water into the boiler to replenish that being used as steam. If the boiler pressure is not steadily rising, the fireman can add more fuel or adjust the air flow through the fire by fully opening the ashpan dampers and fully closing the firedoor.

On locomotives fitted with the Gas Producer Combustion System (GPCS) only the firedoor opening can be adjusted, as the ashpan dampers are normally fixed. On such locomotives it may be necessary to adjust the clinker-control steam to effect an improvement in steam generation. This latter adjustment may not always be available to the locomotive crew, and therefore it may be necessary to request attention from the maintenance staff.

In the case of either conventional or GPCS locomotives there is only a limited ability to deal with poor output from the boiler when the locomotive is working. If the poor output continues it is normally an indication that the fire requires cleaning. Judgement of when the fire requires cleaning (or the grate shaking) is one of the keys skills learned by coal firemen relative to the route they fire over. Too much fire-cleaning will lead to poor fuel economy, whilst too little will lead to poor steaming.

When the driver is about to shut off for a station stop the blower is turned on to prevent the possibility of flames emitting from the firedoor into the cab. As the train comes to rest, the fireman can take two courses of action, depending on the circumstances. If the station stop is only a momentary pause on a long climb, the fireman may increase the blower to keep the fire alive. This keeps the boiler hot and allows for extra water to be put into the boiler if required. If there is already plenty of water in the boiler and/or the station stop is a long one, then the fireman may carefully turn off the blower.

During long station stops or layovers the ashpan dampers and firedoor are closed and the blower is turned off. The fire will then burn through slowly.

Description of oil firing

The expectations placed on the oil fireman tend to be greater than those on his coal-firing counterpart. On oil-fired locomotives in good working order it should be possible to generate the required steam with minimal smoke at the chimney and with minimal steam blowing off through the safety valves. This is because the fire is under fingertip control of the experienced oil fireman. However, this does not mean that oil firing is easy. The oil fireman must be alert at all times, adjusting the controls at precisely the right moment, making judgements on how hard to fire the locomotive and ensuring that a 'flame-out' does not lead to an explosive blowback.

On stepping onto an oil-fired locomotive the fireman will check that the water level is sufficient for the work about to be carried out. If large gradients are ahead, it will be necessary to build up the water level. This is typically carried out during a station stop or gentle coasting. The blower is turned up to provide more draught through the firebox, and simultaneously the oil-control valve and

atomiser are also turned up. This generates more steam and raises the boiler pressure. The fireman can then turn on one of the injectors to force water into the boiler, thus steadily increasing the water level. When the injector is running, the boiler pressure tends to fall due to steam being used to power the injector, and to the influx of cold water. If the fire is turned up sufficiently it is possible for the flame to generate enough excess steam to balance the running of the injector, and the boiler pressure holds steady whilst water is forced into the boiler.

With the fire turned up the locomotive is warmed up ready to work hard. The fireman has to use judgement and increasing experience (of locomotive and route) to choose the right time to turn up the oil settings. If the setting of the fire is turned up too early the fireman must be cautious not to force too much water into the boiler as this can result in priming. Fortunately, with oil firing the flame can be easily turned down, to hold back the boiler pressure from rising. However, the boiler will start to cool down when this occurs.

When the driver opens the regulator the fireman must be ready to make instant adjustments to the fire. In oil-fired locomotives there is no firebed, and thus increased draught through the firebox will suck the flame out if it is too small. The fireman turns up the oil-control valve until the exhaust from the chimney starts to go dark, and then eases back to keep the chimney clear. The atomiser valve is also turned up with the oil. These changes have to be made for every adjustment that the driver makes of the regulator and reverser controls.

When the locomotive is working steadily the fireman checks that the fire is generating a slight excess of steam, shown by a steady rise on the boiler-pressure gauge. The excess steam can then be used to power the injectors and feed water into the boiler to replenish that being used as steam. If the boiler pressure is not steadily rising the fireman can adjust the settings of the oil-control valve and the atomiser. By experimenting with these controls, the steam generation of the locomotive can be increased. If the locomotive is still struggling, the fireman can make a conscious decision to allow gentle smoke to be emitted from the chimney. The increased oil setting can sometimes increase the output from the boiler.

When the driver is about to shut off for a station stop the fireman can take two courses of action, depending on the circumstances. If the station stop is only a momentary pause on a long climb the fireman can turn on the blower before the driver opens the regulator, so that the flame can be kept on a high setting. This keeps the boiler hot and allows for extra water to be put into it if required. If there is already plenty of water in the boiler and/or the station stop is a long one the fireman will not turn on the blower but instead turn the flame right down to its lowest setting as quickly as possible.

During long station stops the oil-control valve and atomiser are turned down as far as possible, so that the flame is just sufficient to maintain the boiler pressure.

If an oil-fired locomotive is to be parked and then left unattended for any time in a siding the burner must be turned out. If this is not done a crosswind could blow out the flame and ultimately cause a blowback when oil vapour reignites. For this reason the crew of oil-fired locomotives should remain within earshot of the locomotive whenever the burner is lit.

Considerations of driving

The driver controls the movement of the locomotive and its train. By skilful use of the regulator and reverser the driver will obtain maximum economy of fuel. On a modern superheated locomotive the driver would opt for a full open regulator wherever possible, and the shortest possible cut-off on the reverser. However, there are many historic locomotives operating on heritage railways that cannot tolerate this type of operation. This may be because of limitations in the mechanical parts, or because they only have saturated boilers (*i.e.* no superheater). The saturated steam will tend to condense if it is expanded too much by very short cut-offs. In either case the regulator may be best operated

with a partial opening, to reduce the steam-chest pressure.

The arrangement for drifting varies greatly between different locomotives, and the driver will need to be familiar with the correct technique to be used with each locomotive. The best way to drift with any given locomotive will be advised by the engineering department of its home railway or owning group. A modern steam locomotive may be most efficiently operated with the reverser in mid gear and with a small drifting steam supply, thus keeping the cylinders warm and minimising wear. A historic locomotive with basic slide valves may be best operated with the reverser in full gear, to obtain an even wear on the slide valves.

It would not be unusual for a driver to encounter both modern and historic steam locomotives on the same railway, and the appropriate techniques for operating each locomotive must be learned.

The braking of long trains requires careful judgement and consideration for what is happening throughout the train and not just on the locomotive. Whether using air or vacuum brakes, the pressure gauges in the cab give the driver a clear indication as to the brake demand being made. The use of various pressure gauges is seen in **Figure 14.1**.

Figure 14.1
The driver prepares for arrival at a station. Notice the various gauges indicating the steam-chest pressure and brake vacuum.

The braking of a long train is not instant, and only through hands-on experience will the driver become familiar with the delay in the brake system. With this increasing experience the driver should become able to stop the train smoothly in the required position by means of minimum changes to the train brake pressure.

The driver requires a good technical understanding of the vehicles in the train to ensure safe operation and to be able to remedy any minor faults. The driver must also be fully conversant with the route, its signalling, speed limits and gradient profiles, the latter being highly important to braking distances and the safe management of the boiler water level. In addition, the driver must thoroughly understand the timetables and the arrangements for train operation, for example single-line working using section staffs, tokens, tickets etc. Only by being fully acquainted with all this knowledge can a driver carry out special workings such as rescuing a failed locomotive or double-heading.

When running round trains and shunting over points that are operated either by adjacent levers or have trailing mechanisms it is important to ensure that the points are set correctly before moving the locomotive over them. This is achieved either by one of the crew getting off the locomotive to check the points or by moving it well clear of the points so that they can be seen from the footplate.

Before a train consisting of any given locomotive and rake of coaches makes its first departure the important brake continuity test must be made. The driver must take care when releasing the brakes for this test and stay with the locomotive. The driver will receive a signal from the guard if the checks are satisfactory.

Whilst the train is on the move the driver should periodically check the motion of the train along the track. The driver puts safety first and the timetable second. There should be no speeding to make up time.

The driver is senior to the fireman and is therefore responsible for the locomotive as a whole including the fireman's duties. With an experienced fireman the driver will generally not interfere with the actions of the fireman, simply observing boiler water levels, smoke at the chimney and providing feedback and support as necessary. With a less experienced fireman the driver will keep a closer eye on the firing of the locomotive and be prepared to assist the fireman with advice, for example during fire cleaning.

Disposal

Chapter 15

Returning 'on shed'

At the end of the day the locomotive returns to the shed and is prepared for the night. The sequence in which the disposal tasks are carried out can vary depending on the common practice of the railway, the condition of the locomotive and also on the preference of the crew. However, following arrival on shed consideration will be given to the following tasks:

1. **Inspect the frames and motion work for loose pins or other faults.**

2. **Start both injectors running in order to fill the boiler with water. As the pressure falls, the injectors will start to struggle, so trim the water feed when necessary to keep the injector working.**

Disposal of a coal fire

The most common procedure is to leave a small fire in the locomotive, which will go out gradually and allow the boiler to cool slowly. The typical procedure for disposal of a coal fire is as follows:

1. **Open the dampers and ensure that there is sufficient space under the firebars for further ash to fall through when the fire is being cleaned.**

2. **Put the blower on and clean the fire to remove ash and clinker. Note that a curved fire iron will help to clean the area underneath the firedoor. As the boiler pressure falls due to injecting water the blower may need to be turned up to continue to be effective. Special care will need to be taken on locomotives with widely-spaced firebars so as not to lose the fire completely through the gaps.**

3. **If possible empty the ashpan. If not, ensure that there is space under the firebars for ash to fall through during the night.**

4. **Ensure that the dampers are firmly closed.**

On locomotives with deep fireboxes an alternative preparation of the fire can be used if the locomotive is required for service again the next day. This is to clean the fire as usual, but to then 'bank up' the fire with coal until it is very deep. Note that it is especially important to have the blower on to prevent blowbacks as the coal ignites. When the fire has been banked up, the firedoor and damper are closed, and the blower can then be turned off. During the night the deep fire will gradually burn through at a steady pace. In addition to keeping the boiler warm until the next day this method simplifies the preparation next morning to cleaning the fire with the fire irons or rocking grate and then adding fresh coal on top.

Shutting down an oil-burner

The process of disposing of an oil-burning locomotive is relatively straightforward, because unlike on coal-fired locomotives there is no need to clean the fire or dispose of ash and clinker. However, the oil fireman must take special care when turning out the burner so as to avoid oil vapour reigniting and causing an explosive blowback. To ensure that such an explosion is avoided, the fireman will follow an approved 'flame-out' procedure. One such procedure is detailed below:

1. **Marginally open the blower.**

2. **Close the oil-shut-off valve.**

3. **Turn off the oil regulator.**

4. Gently open the drain valve; the remaining oil in the burner passages and adjacent pipes should momentarily reignite at the burner.

5. Close the drain valve and operate the purge valve for a few seconds.

6. Open the drain valve fully.

7. Turn off the blower and atomiser.

Disposing of the locomotive

1. Move the locomotive into the shed with its remaining pressure and stop with the chimney under a ventilation duct (if available).

2. Isolate the gauge glasses from the boiler by shutting the top and bottom cocks, so that if the glass breaks during the night it will not drain water from the boiler.

3. Ensure that the firedoor and any intake vents for secondary air are firmly closed.

4. Close all the steam valves. Where isolating valves are fitted to manifolds or steam pipes, these should also be closed.

5. Put the lid on the chimney (where fitted as part of routine).

Before signing off duty the driver should fill in the appropriate log books, additionally recording any faults that will require attention from maintenance staff.

Index